Tell My Sister Where I Am

Tell My Sister Where I Am

Hanhtiet Le and Barbara J. Penner

Tell My Sister Where I am

Published by Hanhtiet Le and Barbara Joanne Penner, Edmonton, Canada

ISBN 0-978-1-77354-184-6

At the request of, and out of respect for individuals in some stories, a few have been renamed.

Photo credits: Hanhtiet and Búp by Tri Kiet Vuong of Kiet's Photo & Studio; Hanhtiet and Barbara by Rachel Berg. Used with permission.

Publication assistance and digital printing in Canada by

PAGEMASTER
PUBLISHING
PageMaster.ca

To Búp and George,
Dan, Cheryl, Corrine, Kelela,
Frank,
Josie and Jacob

*a*cknowledgments

My best, my most excellent sister, Búp, you have loved me through thick and thin. We, like most Vietnamese of our generation, did not grow up hearing or speaking of our love. Now I say with deepest devotion, "I love you, Búp. I have nobody else."

Deborah, my unwavering Canadian friend, you are always there for me.

Mr. Quý Thành, astute giver of insight and advice, to you I owe many, many thanks.

$\mathcal{C}$ontents

Preface

Over the decades, since Deborah, Rudy, and Lydia first drew me in, I have been warmly welcomed by members of the extended family, and close friends. To some I disclosed, from time to time, pieces of my past which weighed me down with anger but mostly pain. Hurtful messages imprinted on me from childhood told me that suffering was my fate, that misery was a sign of my unworthiness, and that the faceless universe had unfolded as it had because it is what it is. I wanted to disentangle myself from such interpretations, all the while longing for causality. I ached to live free from my story. I imagined one day a carefree passing, out from under the weight of it all. Encouraged by caring to share, over many months, I told the recollections recorded here. I have wept and I have laughed till I cried in the retelling. *Cám ơn*, Barbara. It has been healing to unbundle this load. It is good to lay these words down.

Hanhtiet Le

Traipsing onto a Bạch Đằng barge in the bend of the Đồng Nai River above Biên Hòa in 1997, Hanhtiet and I were ferried to the island where she had been born. It was almost Tết, so households were preparing for the stream of well-wishers who customarily dropped by for pumpkin or watermelon seed snacks washed down with cups of tea. Everywhere we went, I drank in the joy of reunions of Hanhtiet and friends unseen for fifteen years or more. The wonderer had returned to a place called home. But the walls of her childhood world had been breached, and beyond, new wonders surfaced. Catching *Tell My Sister Where I Am*, and the other stories springing from Hanhtiet's memory, and staying true to her voice, has engaged us over eight years. Where you hear too much in the key of B, that would be my limping interpretation. It's a rare honour to be invited to bear witness while someone unpacks her recollected roots of character, of dreams both dreadful and splendid, and of hope, faith, and love. Hanhtiet, your confidence has been my on-going reward.

Barbara Penner

Prologue

Earth rises out of ocean forming 3,300 kilometres of coastline that roll into tropical lowlands and pitch upward through steeper terrain peaking on Fan Si Pan 3,144 metres above sea level. From the northern frontier mountains along 23°22' latitude and southward to Cape Ca Mau at 8°33', the sinewy land known as Vietnam lies north of the equator. Except for a few days every December, the sun shines directly overhead someone sweltering below. These measurements and observations come to us courtesy of the fifty-some peoples whose ancestors settled this soil over millenia and whose descendants' blood has been spilled, staining Earth with atrocities peculiar to our own times.

In the 21st century, the Kinh, or Viet people, predominate although, through the current commerce of ideas, their local distinctives are losing ground to global perspectives. During the 20th century, the Vietnamese exchanged more than words with imperialists: American, Chinese, French and Japanese. Hoisted with his own petard, each fell.

Hanhtiet Le, who tells her story here, wasn't yet a twinkle in her father's eye when the French Far East Expeditionary Corps surrendered to the Viet Minh at precipitous Điện Biên Phủ. Following the hasty Geneva Accords of 1954, the temporary military demarcation line along the 17th Parallel hardened into a political boundary. The South, and its Stars and Stripes backers, hadn't signed on in any case. *Lê Bông* was delivered of Hanhtiet subsequent to the "300 days of grace" when roads, rails, and ports were awash with approximately 800,000 internally displaced Vietnamese voting with their feet against the regimes in both Saigon and Hanoi. Two decades on, the aftershocks of that seismic split would best America and cast the seed of the land out upon the waters. What good could come of that?

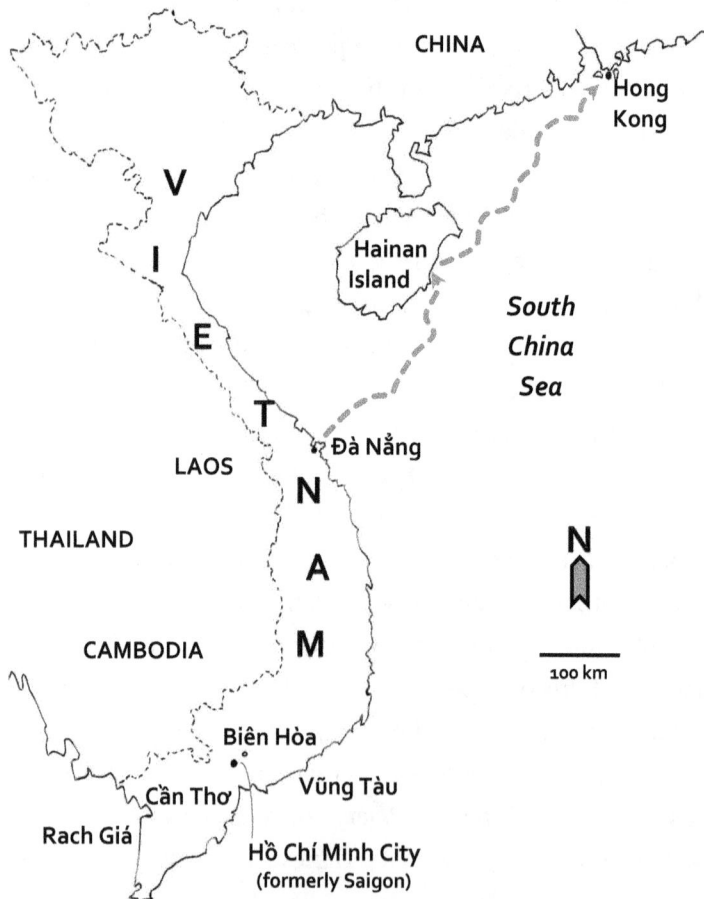

Wonder

The bullet that enters my belly keeps on flying. I sense its exit smidgens before my right hip. With a smack that echoes still, two others sear abrasions across skin, mementos more indelible than tattoos, burning hotter, longer, than the blood pooling beneath my back. Is this the temperature of death? An irregular pulse pounds in my ears almost drowning out the throbbing engine that propels us further into a darkness darker than dark. I pass out, not away. We are going, getting away. Finally. It is the fifteenth of August, 1982. I am floating in and out of consciousness off the coast of *Đà Nẵng*. My fingers find the perforations before my lips find my voice. Faint, my sea-salted tongue calls,

"*Có ai không làm ơn cứu tôi.*"

Somebody... help me.

"*Tôi bị thương.*"

I am hurt.

Does dying come so easily? How effortless is death. Waiting for it, I wonder, not at dying, nor why, nor where my body, once discarded, will descend into the deep, but at living. It fills me, this unfathomable wonder.

So here am I in the middle, but also at both an end and a beginning.

One Quarter, One Half, and All of Me

Cold war rages in grandmother's kitchen. The belligerents, *Bà Ngoại* and *Má*, speak through me to each other when within earshot if they mutter at all. More often than not, silence lasts days, sometimes weeks. This brings a measured, brooding calm in contrast to the high-pitched battles of two women flinging invectives that ricochet off their marks and strike me. Three generations shelter under one roof: one-quarter of me, one-half of me, and all of me within the walls of my world, on an island in the bend of the *Đồng Nai* River.

The river ignores us, the clutch of little boys and a girl born on neighbouring patches of pomelo or sugar cane. There are five or six of us beyond babyhood but before schooling, splashing in the shallows. In my fear of not finding a footing, you could not distinguish me from my shirtless friends in sopping shorts, apart from the ponytail beneath my hat. When I flounder, footholdless, an older cousin seizes my bobbing head and drags me ashore by that hair, alarm in his eyes mirroring panic in my heart. How we envy the eight or ten-year-olds who float with, or paddle into the current, bodies buoyant. They swim, they say smirking condescendingly, courtesy of a dragonfly bite to their belly. As we shimmy along the boughs of a milkfruit tree, my buddy cups a slender insect, transparent wings splay across his tummy which smarts at the sting. Alas, as he drops into the water he still sinks when he kicks his toes toward the surface.

My belly is smooth but for superficial scratches from yesterday's swordfight. Our blades are the sturdy stems of banana leaves which we wield in pretended battle. We fire fictional pistols, index finger aimed and thumb cocked. Scampering after me away from an ambush, Thanh cries, "You're gunned down! Why don't you die?" My breathless laughter provokes and prolongs the conflict. The injustice of the shot falls upon the shooter. That is just war.

Imagine no toys. With bamboo sticks and massive banana fronds, we, the children of South Vietnamese peasants, pass hours constructing forest huts. We smuggle raw rice out of family stashes to cook in condensed milk cans over clandestine fires. What a mash-up of pyromania and hunger! What genius in the plotting and execution! One extracts a recycled tin, another a pocketful of grain, still another a flint; all from under the noses of our chore-mongering mothers. Successful subterfuge whets our appetites for more.

Also sweet is triumph in hitting targets of all types. A most excellent sport is *đánh trổng*. My steady fingers can strike a twig balancing over a pit with such accuracy as to catapult it skyward for my opponent to try to catch in flight. We are devotees of synchronicity, ecstatic at the harmony of hand and eye.

But play is time wrestled from work to which my task master has dedicated me. Around *Tết*, the Lunar New Year, when the sun angles lower over the waters of the *Đồng Nai*,

Grandmother still rises before morning light. Through thin bamboo walls, I hear the crackling flames, the occasional snap of prunings, and I smell burning leaves. The ash fertilizes her precious fruit trees: green thin-skinned oranges, hefty pomelo, and succulent longan. I am not a morning person. I try to squeeze more sleep out of the night. When I stumble to the doorway, ghosts restrain my little legs from stepping over the sill.

"*Bà Ngoại*," my plaintive call floats into the darkness, "Come get me."

Although my grandmother comes muttering, come she does.

"You're a big girl. Still can't do anything by yourself?"

Poking at the fire with a broken branch warms me up. If *Bà Ngoại* has saved a little yam, it can be speared, roasted, and eaten together. There is comfort in being with her, mother of my mother.

Bà Ngoại bears the burden of my earliest wonderings.

Nguyễn Thị Liễu is sixty at my first recollection of her. You would think her scrawny; she is slight but strong and steady. At the nape of her neck, her hair, ever more white than black, is secured in a small knot. Inside the house or out, she usually covers her head with a towel fastened around that bun. This headscarf is replaced by an archetypal conical hat whenever she tends the orchard. Simple cotton trousers and a long-sleeved blouse buttoned to the chin make up her unchanging wardrobe. Equally fixed, but older and more costly, are the single gold rings she wears in each ear.

Those ears hear my many queries. Who could say if my curiosity exceeds that of other youngsters, but one thing is sure, in our household, the monopoly on "why?" is mine. My oft-voiced inquisitiveness is counterbalanced by the right to command, exercised by both mother and grandmother. Over every matter besides putting me in my place, those two are at odds. Common sense and its decades-in-the-making-consequence, wisdom, are exclusively *Bà Ngoại's*. She lets that be known. Therein is the germ of restraint, of my leaving questions unasked. Grandmother's certainty restrains, stifles, constant quizzing lest I reveal the scantiness of my knowledge. I weigh the injustice of ignorance against the sting of mockery that invariably follows my guileless wondering. I decide not knowing is folly and utterly unfair.

A small kid stands in the doorway waiting to be acknowledged. I am that child. I ask as I was asked to.

"My mother's mother says I should get the money from you because payment is two months late."

The neighbour who is in debt to my mother's mother may say nothing, ignoring my tiny and powerless presence. She may shoo me away. Nine times out of ten I trip home empty-handed. This feels like a punishment. Back at grandmother's house, I have nothing to give her. Before she sent me, she knew there would be no repayment. This I know.

I don't know how much is enough. I am holding out a two-handled cooking pot. A fistful of raw rice grains roll around the bottom of it. *Bà Ngoại* peers inside.

"How senseless can you be, daughter of my daughter? That's not enough for you and me, let alone for three."

"You said a few grains."

"Three tin can measures!"

A trio of three-legged ceramic stoves sit on the cooking platform in our kitchen. I clear the ashes and arrange the kindling to start the fire beneath one stove. The platform is higher than my chest. I push a stool next to the stoves and arrange the pot with sufficient rice, now rinsed and settled one-knuckle-deep in well water. I climb down and light the fire. Keeping the flame consistent is beyond me. At the next meal I hear the crunch of raw kernels between my teeth, the spoon scraping at the burned bits and *Bà Ngoại's* complaints about my stupidity to *Má*. Meals are better when *Bà Ngoại* is neither too ill nor too busy in her orchard to do the cooking.

Grandmother's orchard is her dominion. She works it knowledgeably and well. She works herself. She works me too. In the dry season, from November to April or May, we haul water up the well shaft, fill pails carried by yoke to every tree, day after day. My child-sized hoe is no toy; weeding is serious business. I think my labour entitles me to an orange. Grandmother's wish-squelching look sends a definitive "No!"

A sudden sound, deep and low, sends me scurrying to *Bà Ngoại*. She can scarcely peel my limbs from her legs. We hear a traditional drum; the beating of the taut water buffalo hide reverberates throughout the neighbourhood calling youngsters to school. Its primal pulse alarms me almost as much as the squealing of male piglets under the knife of the castrator. When his bicycle horn wheezes at our gate, I pale and flee, damming my ears.

Beyond the bamboo walls of the house, I hear crickets whose unceasing chirping wanes only at twilight, overwhelmed by whirring wings backed by a chorus of croaks from frogs most intense in the rainy season. The bull frogs' bass booms out then, when it's windy, cool, and melancholy. These melodies play on and on throughout my childhood – nature's mood music, orchestral Asia, inimitable. In borrowed voices of domestic animals: a cat, a dog, a duck, or a water buffalo, my pals and I signal to each other readiness to play, or that grownups have restricted our mobility. We code-switch to evade detection by adult ears.

An occasional co-conspirator in my pre-school days is my half-sister. *Má* married *Búp*'s father in the heady days when the Japanese were being swept from Vietnam, and the Viet Minh were denying the returning French a seamless resumption of hegemony over Indochina. *Búp* can't recall her father; within weeks of her birth he lost his life battling imperialists bent on *la mission civilisatrice*. She remembers my father agreeing to have her under his roof when he wed *Má*. But *Bà Ngoại* over-ruled so *Búp* remained primarily a labour-slaving grand-daughter rather than becoming an under-foot step-daughter. *Má's* second husband departed too, about a year into their union, though not lost to death but to some unspoken other life. Then *Má* reappeared at *Bà Ngoại's* door with me, her second father-less daughter.

Familial relations with *Búp*'s paternal grandparents persist and her many cousins like lugging toddler me about. They pinch my chubby cheeks and pitch me head-first when I wriggle and writhe in their own juvenile clutches. A gash in my forehead earns me no sympathy from *Má* who swats me for getting into trouble.

"Why won't you shield me from these tyrants?" my inarticulate three-year-old self gibbers.

When the kids traipse out among the water buffalo, the others sense my fearlessness and set me astride a young calf. Almost immediately I'm bucked off, flying into the water hole. I am not amused. The others double up at the sight.

"Not a word of this to *Má*," Búp shushes me, "or I won't bring you along anymore."

This is the first of many sister pacts.

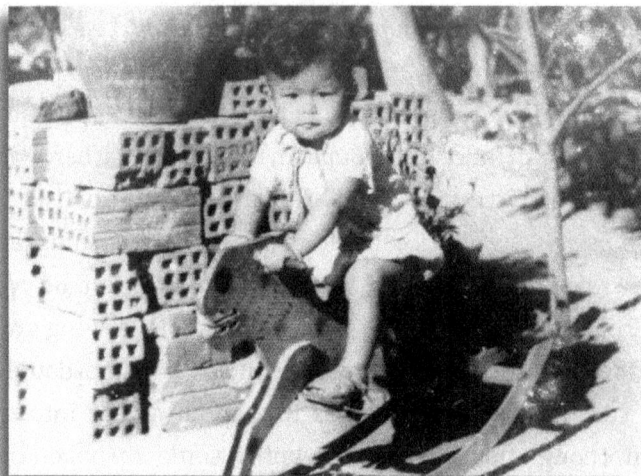

Hanhtiet, 1958, Grandmother's orchard

At the Lunar New Year, *Búp* includes me in a visit to her city cousins in *Biên Hòa*, forty-five minutes by motor cycle south east of *Mỹ Quới* Island. I wait by the gap in the flowering shrubbery where the dapper young fiancé of an aunt has parked his bicycle. It's all glint and glimmer. I'm a big-mouth pest but he, still in the impress-the-girl stage, succumbs to my charms and I wheedle more speed out of him.

"Could you take me to your house, Uncle? I've never seen it, Uncle. You ARE my uncle, right, Uncle?"

"You asked your big sister?"

"Oh, yes!" I lie.

On the back carrier, right flip flop pressed to the chain stay, I wrap my arms around Uncle's waist and ride with glee through the streets of the provincial capital. When we reach his silent house, he seats me in the salon and tells me to wait. My eyes drink in the beauty of ornate, wooden furniture, polished to sheen. I spy a bowl of unfamiliar fruit almost as lustrous as the table it is sitting on. I have never seen apples before; their green, golden and rosy skins are oh, so smooth. I finger a stem and glance around. Uncle is out of sight. My teeth pierce the thin skin of a yellowish one; the flesh seems mushy. I put it back in the bowl, tiny teeth marks down. The texture of a red apple has a little more crunch; I munch and swallow, then return this one too, discreetly placing the bitten patch on the bottom. I pinch a green one and rearrange the platter so it looks untouched.

Back at our cousins', I tell *Búp* I've tasted a new fruit. Later we learn Uncle suspects mice in his house; something small has been nibbling apples.

"There! There's your mouse!" my sister laughs, outing me, exposing my thievery.

When the adults leave *Bà Ngoại's* property, I am left on security detail. My five year-old eyes suspect ghosts in every shadow. I sit in the spotted shade of leafy fruit boughs and hear the neighbour boys meowing beyond the hedge. The call to accompany them appeals to my small and lonely self. I leave. I leave our family's assets unguarded. *Bà Ngoại* comes back and finds no one at home. In my absence, her vexation steeps. My return, silent and subdued, is neither sufficiently quiet nor quiescent. *Bà Ngoại* summons me. I tiptoe to her and stand straight but small, staring at my ten toes lined up taut in the sand. Her lecture on disobedience rains down on me. I cannot tell her how little I feel, how impossible it would be for me to resist a burglar should one come. *Bà Ngoại's* voice is stern, her face severe, and in her grip is steel. She squats, wielding a kitchen cleaver in a chopping motion over my feet, touching my toes. She raises the blade. It hovers, about to ...

"I will chop off your feet so you cannot run off again."

Wide-eyed fear holds my breath. *Bà Ngoại* swings. UUGH! The knife-edge bites into earth far from my quaking feet. I am flabbergasted by my grandmother's abysmal aim.

"You didn't do a very good job," my cheeky self thinks and as the tension snaps, I am overtaken by fits of laughter.

Bà Ngoại cannot contain herself at the sight of her hysterical granddaughter. She too doubles over. Till tears drip from our chins, we laugh and laugh and laugh together.

And at night we sleep together. My small fingers reach out for the draw string at the waist of the trousers *Má* or *Bà Ngoại* wear. Sleep comes only when I am attached by this cord to the women to whom I owe my life. Bad habit that it is, mother or grandmother bats my hand.

Má whines, "Why? Let go!"

But *Bà Ngoại's* own instincts are activated in the darkness; her feet, her toes, are in incessant motion as if she's chasing Moon through her phases in the sky. Is she awake or asleep? When does she rest?

There is no snoozing at the New Moon Festival in August. This is the moon of the pomelo harvest. Under a clear, inky sky, Earth is drenched in silver. In preparation, *Bà Ngoại* peers past the leaf-shine to the golden citrus orbs hanging twenty or twenty-five feet up. My sights soar to the billions of stars blinking beyond. I scramble up the tree trunks. Beneath me, *Bà Ngoại* points out several specific fruit. With both hands, I hold and turn to twist each pomelo off its stem. These samples are sold to a fruit merchant who buys an entire crop and sends a crew to pick our orchard. Citrus trees are easier on climbers than coconut palms. There is an art to binding moist banana stalks into a circle and twisting it into a figure eight around a palm trunk. This banana band protects my feet as I shimmy it all the way up to the top. There, above the leafy canopy, I see roofs of neighbouring homes poking up through the island of green within the perimeter of the clear currents of the *Đồng Nai*. These trees house all manner of birds. The boys I climb with like to poke around in their nests. They retrieve eggs but I avoid the featherless not-yet fledglings; touching their sticky, bony bodies makes my skin crawl.

Plumage of another sort itches *Bà Ngoại*. At least that's how she perceives her greying hair. I am employed to extract white ones and I negotiate my wages. Twenty hairs are worth a pittance. Fifty earns me a banana. Does *Bà Ngoại* see the bald spot I leave behind? Does she feel me yank sheaves rather than single strands when a mock duck gawk-gawks from behind the house?

Before I am permitted to play, there are daily chores to be done. As Vietnam unveils her face to the sun, about 6 o'clock, the concrete-like clay floor must be swept.

"Look at you. You don't know how to bend your back." Grandmother critiques my technique with the home-made straw broom. When *Má* does the sweeping, *Bà Ngoại's* eyes spy dust loitering along every wall.

"Ah, your mother swept," she sighs. "She only touched 'the highway'".

It is everlasting, this sweeping, what with walls of bamboo. My grandparents' home originally had an exterior skin of solid wood but the flood of the '40s washed it away. The load-bearing center wall remains, within a cluster of rooms. Dark and weighty chairs and a table burnished by years of polishing occupy the public room. There are two chambers for sleeping and the kitchen lean-to.

The kitchen is where I bring the catch-of-the-day once I learn to fish. In rainy season, the high-water mark reaches road level. Dense or daring, river fish swim into canals and ditches dug around the farms and orchards. They hide among hay stalks and consider themselves concealed among grasses but the sun sears overhead and the waters subside, trapping catfish, mudfish or river cobbler inland. I wade into sludge, knee or thigh deep. Kids like me build barriers and engineer primitive locks, emptying section by section with buckets. In the reservoirs, we stir up the sludge which the fish can't abide. As they float to the surface, we seize them in our bare hands. My angler's heart thrills at eight or ten days of unceasing rain. I anticipate an excellent haul. Fish in my can is money in my hand. Whenever I catch many, I peddle dozens door to door in the neighbourhood. We also stow some in ceramic jugs where the fish sluggishly swish their fins for five or six days before being cooked. One fish feeds two women and one girl for a day. Bringing home protein boosts my own merit. The chives, shallots, red chili peppers, tomatoes, suey choy, and bamboo shoots we eat all grow in our vegetable plot. Pineapples are often on the table because another fruit forms whenever one is taken, whatever the season. My catch, together with our other mainstay, rice, completes a meal.

$\mathcal{P}$utting Two and Two Together

The seasons of my life shifted dramatically in 1962. Living in the moment of a timeless present was overtaken by measured passages. I entered the first grade, one of about fifty untamed six and seven-year olds corralled from all over the island in one room with one teacher straining under the burden of schooling us. She could not handle, let alone help all of us. The smart ones surged ahead by their own wits. I did not. I knew I was failing to learn. Anxiety coalesced around my confusion. School scared me. My sole pleasure was being among peers, although turning the tables on the child to adult ratio utterly distracted me. Most constant was the feeling of being tugged, yanked even, in different directions. I finished the year as I had begun, unable to read or write. I became a repeater. Yet this reprise opened my eyes. I realized that neither *Bà Ngoại* nor *Má* knew the inside of the school from the out. I saw some neighbours, heads bent over books. Could they unlock the secrets of learning? On their advice, I bowed before the teacher, copy book in hand. Would she make dotted-line-letters for me to trace? Perhaps for the first time, an adult truly saw me as a girl with a hungry mind. And I began observing patterns on paper and imitating the plump letters of Vietnamese handwriting, scratched at first but eventually flowing from the stubby lead pencil in my chubby fingers.

The *Đồng Nai* was my first great teacher. Like a fish, and liking fish, I loved the river's breezy coolness. As a seven and eight year-old, I was on her banks as often as possible. That's where people would find me, not just immersed when one hundred percent humidity slicked cloth to skin and air hung heavy in one's lungs, but guiding my rods to still waters. The island's lush vegetation was colonized by various species of ants. *Bà Ngoại* taught me that the yellow wingless weaver ants protected her fruit from agricultural pests. Their nests were my source for the best fish bait. Hanging high above me in the orchard was an orb of leaves, as large as a human head, engineered into overlapping layers sealed with the insects' secretions. Probing and poking it with a sharpened stake, I caught lumps of larvae as they tumbled down into my basket. For fishing rods, I had two bamboo poles, one long, one short. Along a nylon line, I secured a floater made from a buoyant corn cob tip. Below the hook, thick with gummy insects, I knotted a sinker to weight the lure low into the pools.

Mud oozing between my toes, I learned the correlation between the canopy above and my chances of a catch below. Beneath leafy boughs or in high water, I could fling a fish on a short rod up into the air without losing it, reel-less as I was. My longer pole worked well under open skies where shallow waters didn't require me to hoist a heavy catch too high. Before settling on a site, I read the river's surface for tell-tale signs of the current carrying whatever I was trawling for. Eyes and hands sensed unseen prey playing with the bait. Sometimes the floater began bobbing as fish nibbled the larvae; the tactics of other fighters were signaled by a suddenly sinking corn cob. With intensity, the entire rod needed to be whipped skyward. Too soon, too rapid a movement and I would lose the contest. My fingers measured the motion and muscle of my contender. In those days, the *Đồng Nai* was teeming with fish and it didn't take long to fill my basket. But time didn't count.

Patience, now that paid dividends for the shrimp tracker. Perched on slender legs, a prawn approached my lure more intelligently than its finned and faster friends. When my bobbin began to sway in the water, I knew the pincers of a slender crustacean tentatively held the bait. The deeper the bow in my bamboo, the larger the could-be catch. I had to let them run a little, those shrimp, before snagging them with a deft jerk. And still, some eluded me.

All through my primary school years, I'd scoop up the rods resting on *Bà Ngoại's* hibiscus hedge and head to the river several times a day. I basked in the wealth of the water. Out from under the suppression of our household of unhappiness, solitude soothed me there on the river bank. *Đồng Nai's* tranquility contrasted with the hot-tempered women from whom I would sneak away. Concentrating on looping nylon, or decoding the messages pulsing along the line into my fingers, unknotted my mind. I started to read predictable patterns in people too. Whenever I slunk home empty-handed, I would feel a wrathful hand but if I returned with fish, the cloud would lighten. My education was proceeding. I was putting two and two together.

Meanwhile acts of war were multiplying. Greedy hands tossed readily-available grenades into riverside depths. Stunned, scathed and lifeless fish floated easy gain into shrewd wallets leaving less for just-enough-to-fill-a-stomach fishers like me. A South Vietnamese military post was built next to our local school. The lookout tower loomed over the yard. Barbed wire encircled newly-dug defense trenches topped with sandbags packed square around rifle slots. Sandbags appeared inside our house too. *Bà Ngoại* prepared a shelter under her solid, wooden daybed. Jute sacks filled with sand and banana tree trunks buttressed the furniture which I saw first as a fortress to play or nap in. One night, however, *Má* shook me awake and hustled me within the earthen walls while *Bà Ngoại* flung more sandbags on the top before scrambling in after us. Gunshots. Shouts. Grenades. Explosions. My bladder could not hold.

Morning came. I walked, as usual, toward school along the perimeter fence of the army post. On the barbs, I saw shreds of skin. Snagged on the wire: a severed hand, a shock of hair in a chunk of skull. Then a pair of hips and legs. In the ditch, on the road, more unidentifiable body parts. Inside the wire, soldiers waited. Outside, villagers lingered, looking for the authorities. I had never seen an intact corpse before, let alone fragments of dismembered bodies. These I see in my mind, even now. I see the dead. I never, never, ever walked that kilometre to primary school alone again. For four more years, I took that road only in the company of classmates.

By the fifth grade, I was sturdy and agile on my feet. They carried me everywhere. Then my half-sister brought a bicycle from the city. *Búp* was ten years my senior and had been working in Saigon since I was a pre-schooler. The second-hand adult-sized bike had been hers before she gave it to me. I reached up to the hand grips and pushed it, circling the house. All the blood drained from my fists. It was exhausting watching the spokes cycle by while my short legs plodded past the empty pedals. I tried hoisting the bike up the two steps into the shade by the door. My school books fit neatly into the spring-loaded carrier behind the saddle. How I longed to ride! Sitting on the crossbar with the frame leaning against a tree wasn't at all satisfying. On tiptoes, I pushed the bike forward. While hopping on one foot, I pedaled with the other until I reached enough momentum to press both feet onto the rubber. Over and over, I would tip and crash into the sand. The bruising didn't hurt quite as much as *Má's* refusal to help me balance. I had seen her cycling successfully on a borrowed bike and knew she had the knack, but she wouldn't reach out to steady the frame until I got up to speed. Perhaps I had absorbed some of *Má's* perpetual disparagement of *Búp's* material support; *Má* viewed both her daughters as substandard sources of income. Maybe my inability to operate the far-too-big bicycle accentuated my sense of inadequacy. Feeding my misery, I told myself *Búp* disliked the bike and conveniently cast it off on me. In fact, *Búp* had my future in mind. She anticipated that, like she had, I was reaching a crossroads where *Má's* way of life and mine would part.

There were other paths to follow. Cow carts rumbled along island trails loaded with freshly cut cane. A sugar baron built a processing plant and warehouse on the island. Upstream boats delivered the tall sweet stems while freighters eased up the estuary for sugar bricks. The first electric lights in the district enabled round-the-clock production; local adults found employment, the kids entertainment. Along with other children, I whiled away hours watching the extraction. Cane juice pooled in massive vats, was boiled, filtered, sprinkled with white powder and boiled again to clarified gold. Parents of schoolmates stirred the viscous syrup with long wooden paddles and poured batches into countless bamboo frames. Once set, these blocks of crystalized sugar could be popped out of the molds with just the right thumb pressure. To me, this was play and, although the high temperature of the liquid gold raised the risk of burns, I loved to participate as permitted. I chewed on scrap cane and observed the particular precision with which beautiful sugar blocks set on straw in wooden boxes were stacked and stored. Where were all those amber granules in all those crates in all those ships going? I marvelled.

Much more than sugar was flowing along the *Đồng Nai* in 1968. More than the usual fireworks exploded at the Lunar New Year on January 31. The *Tân Uyên* area was rife with *Việt Cộng* sympathizers and supporters, both voluntary and 'voluntold'. *Thuế* in the form of rice or medicine was expected when night-time knocking signaled the VC were outside the door. If you didn't hand over the ask at the first request, a more insistent and forceful knock would be heard later. Shadowy voices appealed to patriotism.

"This is our quest for liberty. The French and then the Americans invaded our country, colonized, plundered, and are destroying us. Together, we sacrifice ourselves for freedom; we bleed, you feed."

It was the same contribution the South Vietnamese government collected on the other side of sunrise. Poverty-stricken farmers bent low under doubly heavy levies; the lack of men in *Bà Ngoại's* household spared us from the definitive demand for bone of our bones, a brother or a son. But bombs or bazookas, whether launched from tunnels or plummeting from helicopters, burned with equal intensity. Infernos blazed and choking black smoke billowed from bamboo thickets, thatched roofs or flaming fields of rice. The ferry footpath outside my grandmother's gate filled with running parents, kids on backs or babies in arms.

In the thick of it, I asked, "Are we going?"

"Where to?"

Má and *Bà Ngoại* had no answers. Other than hearsay from neighbours, there was no source of news about troop movements, skirmishes with guerillas or casualties. Radio-less, our isolation from wartime propaganda also cut us off from festive *Tết* programming.

School resumed after the New Year's vacation with absolutely no discussion of the *Tết* Offensive; the walls had ears. We all hunkered down, like most of our neighbours, until the next round.

Let Fate Not Fall

Around the bend of years, ways diverged for us island children. Grade Five students sat the national secondary school entrance examinations. Ten kilometres from my home, on the east bank of the river, was the district public high school. Secondary education was a privilege in 1968; competition to secure a seat was fierce. I walked two hours in the shadow of my classmate's father who willed his own daughter to succeed. Challenging this hurdle was the first independent ambition of mine - a lonely, little girl determined to find a future beyond the confines of fate.

We wrote entrance exams from morning to late afternoon. As I headed home, I was unsure of the results. The grades were to be posted at the same site but I did not know how to find my way back. I was convinced that studying was my only way to a vaguely understood better life. If I failed, *Má* would not pay fees at a private secondary. That would be the end of my book learning. A few days later my classmate cycled by the orchard.

"Hanhtiet! You passed! You got in! And I did too!"

My body responded, springing from earth. My hands and feet flew skyward. In ecstasy, I leapt about the yard. I could not sound the depths of my joy. I, whose ears so often heard,

"Stupid girl. You're useless," had come to see myself as such. But that message was a lie. Against all odds, I had struggled and would struggle not to perpetuate the poverty of my mother, a landless labourer, without ambition and careless of tomorrow. By age eleven, I was perceiving a pattern of laziness and lack in our village: no education, no knowledge, and no defense against exploitation by those with fistfuls of gold, or simply fists, under their control. A life like *Má's* held no appeal. To grow up, to wed, to serve in-laws, to birth babies, to eke out subsistence, to stay the karmic course, to stifle curiosity, to all this my response was "How can I get out?"

There was no one to answer. *Bà Ngoại*, font of wisdom though she was, was illiterate. I had asked her the big questions of morality, the why of social obligations, and the how of behaviour as a guest or as a gardener. She judged me untrustworthy at such a menial task as fertilizing pomelo trees. Being unreliable, or even worse, deceitful, meant I was unworthy to profit from my labour. Though for years I had been at her side hauling water to the seedlings, the fruit was not mine for the taking. Visiting cousins who had never lifted a bucket were offered the best fruit. Sometimes, when Grandmother wasn't at home, I'd select an excellent citrus specimen, hide and devour it. This I considered my right. As for the longan whose thin boughs and fragile branches I climbed to slip protective paper wrappers around drupes, peckish birds weren't the only raiders. As I circled round the trees keeping an eye on swirling wings overhead, the phenomenal fragrance lured me.

"What are you doing there?" *Bà Ngoại* would shout out omnisciently from the shade.

I thought I was a cunning crook, plucking only a few luscious longan from the skyward side of a cluster so she wouldn't notice any gap. But when accused, my denials fell flat. The scent of mandarin on my breath, longan juice dried between my fingers, or pomelo peel under my nails gave me away. "Impenetrable rind," *Bà Ngoại* quoted, "yields to sharpened fingernails."

Or she would cluck, "A child's mind is a child's mind."

But I wasn't an entirely immature mind in the body of a peasant granddaughter. Up until then, I had felt like other countryside kids, and I don't suppose much would have distinguished me from my peers. At *Lễ Vu Lan*, the mid-summer Veneration of Mothers Day, the stem of a rose was pinned to the lapels of people crowding the temple grounds. One massive lotus-positioned Buddha smiled enigmatically, entirely calm and contemplative amid the flurry of kids clanging metal rods on tiny saucers. Three-score of us rhythmically beat these *mõ* as we chanted in unison under the distracted direction of a lay priest. Most of us were entirely without formal religion though animist superstitions coloured many of our practices. Once a year we lit incense sticks and chanted unintelligible blessings on our mothers. In honour of living *Má*, my rose was red. White petals paid homage to mothers taken too early. I wasn't questioning the centuries-old Confucist perspective that age was owed honour. However, in revering elders, I was becoming quite selective. Those who knew more became soul models for me; from them I gleaned both how and what to learn.

During the late rainy season school recess, island pre-teens became peanut harvesters. Long before dawn, I roused myself.

Sometimes *Bà Ngoại* already had rice boiling. Into a softened, flexible strip of banana leaf, I pressed rice, dried fish, cucumber, and fish sauce. This lunch and a canister of boiled water went into a wide woven bamboo basket which I carried on one hip. In my other hand, I held a glass bottle; glowing within was a burning wad of tightly wound cotton soaked in paint thinner. By four in the morning, several such torches were bobbing along footpaths to the ferry. The boatman motored my friends and me to the *Lợi Hoà* bank where we began our trek to the peanut fields. For ten to fifteen kilometres, the slapping of our flip flops against the soles of our feet provided the beat to the warbling of songbirds, barking of dogs, gapping of geese and crowing of roosters as the eastern sky reddened. By then, farmers who needed labourers were out and about, calling to passersby.

"You looking to pick peanuts? Come! Work!"

And work for peanuts we did. We learned to negotiate our pay before being sent into a field. As sharecroppers, we would bargain for one to six or one to five payment in peanuts; on a good day we'd head home with our baskets as heavy as our twelve-year-old muscles could carry. Farmers designated ripened rows and we spaced ourselves two arm-widths apart working our way across a field over several hours. As we pulled up the knee-to-thigh-high plants, we piled them neatly, stalks and leaves to one side, ground nuts to the other. Our bare toes dug into the earth as our backs bent, fingers bundled around three plants. Both hands drew the best and biggest pods up through crumbly soil. At mid-day, we gathered, five or six friends and strangers with the same sand under our fingernails, to eat our packed lunches - as long as roving cats or dogs hadn't helped themselves first. Outside, under slightly overcast skies, savouring aromatic rice, licking tangy traces of fish sauce off my lips was bliss. Here was I on Earth. I lay back, tracking frothy clouds across the sky and I let my imagination go. What was beyond those lofty wisps and heaven-obscuring billows? Who might be behind the haze? Such questions I asked no one, just wondered.

I abandoned myself to awe. I saw human beings infinitesimally tiny against the vastness of the universe. A light breeze settled my soul. In such moments, I felt free of the adults who kept my curiosity in check at home. *Má* paid my development no heed. *Bà Ngoại's* love and care for me were sometimes cryptic. She couldn't cope with my candid questions. How often had I read incredulity in her face at the nonsensical tangents of my mind? I turned my probing words inward but willed my eyes wider to see more, to look, to learn.

Over a week or two of daily forays to the peanut farms, I carried home enough nuts to last until next year's crop. It took three bright days out under the sun for the pods, spread on banana stalk mats, to sufficiently dry. Once all sand or mud crumbled off, the pods were returned to darkness. *Bà Ngoại* stored our annual supply in large ceramic urns in a shadowy corner of the house. The peanuts, along with fish, roasted or in soup, provided protein in our diet. Shelled and boiled, the nuts made a satisfying snack as *Bà Ngoại* and I sat under her awning in the August twilight.

Despite all my contributions to the family pantry, I was still an expensive child. Whereas two-thirds of my local classmates left school that year for manual and usually menial labour, earning a few *đồng* to add to their household income, my entering sixth grade at the district high school meant a uniform had to be made. Until then, in the primary grades, any button-up blouse and trousers were acceptable. The five local girls going on with our education went to a seamstress who sewed us each an *áo dài* with *Tân Uyên* High School embroidered on a label over the collar bone. The form-fitting, long-sleeved top was uncomfortable and hot. Its flowing, knee-length front and back panels designed to modestly conceal female legs were utterly impractical when pedalling a bicycle. Tying the "tails" at my hip enabled movement but strained respectability. In requisite white, the *áo dài* needed daily laundering, although in my case, once a day wasn't always enough. Asking for soap became one more flashpoint between *Má* and me.

During the dry season, riding the now-mastered bicycle along rice paddy dikes to school cut the travel time in half. Once the rains came, paths degraded under buffalo hooves. I attempted to manoeuver my way, wobbling around puddles and ended up in paddy. By the time I reached the island's east ferry where I stowed my bike, I was filthy. I waded into the river and rinsed the mud out of my clothing. The wind above the water whisked away the wet during the crossing. Half an hour later I arrived at school feeling, yet again, a bedraggled rustic among townsfolk. Over the months, we five island girls wisened up and made a deal with *Tân Uyên* classmates. We would carry our uniforms to their homes and be permitted there to change out of, or into, splashed or sopping traveling clothes.

Life lessons demanded critical thinking unlike most learning activities of the fifty students crammed into a sixth grade classroom. Sometimes thinking at all was too much. In mathematics we were subject to the ill-tempered principal whose violent reactions to misunderstandings or mistakes scared me stiff. If I couldn't compute at the chalkboard, would he slap my face or put boot to my butt?

"Whatever have you been eating at home? You fool! You'll never grasp these formulas!" As he raged, his apoplectic face purpled. Our eyes bulged. Our minds emptied. I was mortified when my bladder wouldn't hold. Embarrassment and anxiety combined to box me into geometric ignorance.

The notorious principal was an anomaly. Other secondary school instructors approached their students with love and their classes with enthusiasm. This was the year the English language was introduced. Since the Vietnamese alphabet shares twenty-two Latin letters with English, silent reading came easily. In class or at home in the evenings, bent over my copybook, I wrote and re-wrote the vocabulary lists and verb conjugations sealing all the spellings and suffixes in my brain. All our tests were paper-based and a good memory served me well. There was no need to apply the language. We listened as our teacher explained *English for Today* in Vietnamese. Her voice animated characters Mr. Brown and Mrs. Black in conversations which we parroted back in chorus. Apart from those dialogue scripts, English words never crossed our lips that year.

Real, live English-speakers rarely appeared at school. From time to time, American teams provided rudimentary medical and dental care. After enduring a toothache, I got to see an American up close and personal. During the extraction, I concentrated on the impossibly blond and curly eyelashes blink, blink, blinking a few inches away from mine. Very hairy forearms shimmered in the sunlight as the medic flicked beads of sweat off his face instead of patting forehead and neck as we did with our ever-present hankies.

The proximity of our school to a military base may have encouraged that kind of "hearts and minds" campaign. Only once in my school years did the army presence put our class in jeopardy. In seventh grade, I was in an English class being instructed by a guest American when an ear-splitting explosion sent kids shrieking under furniture, pee dribbling. The American drew a hidden revolver and poised to fire out through the doorway. A school administrator clattered up the corridor. The white man vanished. We children were herded away from exterior walls and doors. A couple more thunderous detonations shook the nearby base under *Việt Cộng* fire but the school wasn't a target. Classes resumed without further ado within thirty minutes ... as if we hadn't been rocked by bombs before ... as if a childhood pocked by adult anger management issues wasn't fissuring us profoundly...

My second year at secondary, a new principal took charge, bent on raising the reputation of the school academically and athletically. Classes included track and field, volleyball, basketball or ping pong just two hours a week, but at every break the dusty badminton court became my space to perfect self-control. My naturally fidgety feet kept me loose and limber anticipating my opponent's next move. Drop shots, fast and slow, clear shots, smashes fore and back, serving, popping, driving, all these skills and strategies energized me. Pacing myself and analyzing angles of return, I sized up the player opposite. I interchanged grips to keep the shuttle flying to my target. Intramural success opened the way to intercollegiate competition. Principal *Tây* defended absence from core subjects to ensure *Tân Uyên* brought home the pennants. He also provided any missed lessons to keep his athletes in the game scholastically. After off-campus matches, we often crowded into his office for catch-up sessions in chemistry, geography, literature or whatever gap needed filling.

Seeing the dedication of many teachers, I gave my all. I couldn't contemplate the high price of failure in any subject. I ventured to expose my Achilles heel to *Quang*, the ever-patient mathematics instructor and my physical education coach.

"Last year geometry was beyond me," I confessed.

He, like every staffer and student, was well aware of our former principal's mean methods. Teacher *Quang's* explanations untangled my anxiety-riddled approach to computations and calculations.

For centuries in Vietnam, the unschooled had venerated the scholar. The seriousness with which most of our teachers took their responsibilities to develop mind, body and spirit gave them a nobility above even the most revered parents. Six days a week, we spent more waking hours with instructors than with family. They were highly-regarded guardians of our best interests who, when chaperoning a school trip, upheld the strictest social mores by sleeping outside the doorway of the girls' quarters lest any male dare come close.

Despite the profusion of young men in uniform, of guerilla goings-on, and military manoeuvres, local officials organized sports and musical meets. Dressed in our district colours, twenty to thirty kids piled into the back of military trucks, perched on equipment bags and instrument cases, bouncing along thirty kilometres west into rubber plantation country. Choirs belted out patriotic tunes. The propaganda value of love of country, pride in combat, and glory of independence faded as we promptly forgot contrived lyrics. Unforgettable, however, was the hastily added swimming competition for which two girls were conscripted when Principal *Tây* discovered none of our boys were good in the water. The reservoir was big.

"Too wide for me," I tried unconvincingly to weasel out of the contest.

"Just try."

"If you lose, it's no big deal, but we're rooting for you!"

The shoreline cheering section roared in my ears as I splashed my way to the distant waterfront. Victory came with one thousand piasters! I handed my surprising prize to our administrator. It covered half my extracurricular fees for the year. We all celebrated *Tân Uyên's* champs from field to bandstand. Around the evening campfire, and wrapped in an army-issue blanket on a grass mat inside the tent our team had pitched, my mind replayed the events of the day. My intense sense of belonging was altogether surreal.

In contrast, *Má's* pressure on me to abandon books really intensified as I reached fourteen years of age.

"What good will schooling do you? I can count the scholars who don't even have coins in their pockets to tally."

Má looked at my sturdy, strong body and saw packets of potential pay coming her way. School consumed six to eight hours of my day. To avoid *Má's* harangue, I hired myself out to a neighbour whose barge transported sand or gravel for construction. I became a coolie each evening, lugging by yoke four cubic metres of wet, heavy soil by the light of the rising moon. My first contract netted me bruised and swollen shoulders and a few piasters to pay for textbooks. The boss let me off to recover but rehired me ten days later. When I came home for supper, *Má's* dissuasion studded every sentence.

"Here she is, the girl who knows how to eat but not make money. Look at neighbour Mrs. *Ba's* son and Mr. *Bai's* daughter. They bring their wages to their parents."

My mother's pique at shelling out rather than raking in coin from daughter number two was amplified by daughter one's presumed withholdings. My elder sister *Búp* hadn't brought city-earned wages to the island in almost two years; she had heard more than enough of *Má's* carping. Just when my heart was so weighed down that I despaired of ever graduating, a relative heading for Saigon agreed to take me along. Two million strong, the city throngs engulfed us and astonished me. Surprised at my showing up unannounced, *Búp* nevertheless pulled me close and filled me with city fare: steamy wontons and saucy noodles. I trailed behind her through the market where she replaced my threadbare clothes and pressed a packet of cash into my pocket. Before directing me home, my big sister promised to send money for school supplies; this she did although we couldn't hide it from *Má* for long. Then the tirade about me being all liability and no credit to her ratcheted up a notch.

Also escalating was the war. Mandatory military service lurked just around the turn of years for the schoolboys in my classes. We saw numbers of senior-class men dwindle. Still, school discussions skirted the elephant in the room. I felt the weight of worry. We all kept to proven paths, never exploring beyond the periphery of the known, and shuddered under gunship sorties. When death or injury struck a classmate's home or household, we made a donation or chipped in for a floral funeral arrangement. These were compassion's socially acceptable ways and bound us together, but only loosely.

Personal pain or shame wasn't shared. Through all my school years, I felt inferior due to my family dynamics. I imagined that all my classmates' homes were loving. Comments here and there that mother had given them this or that, or that father had bought even a teeny thingamajig confirmed the peculiarity of my family. *Má* didn't show love like other mothers; something was wrong with me, I concluded. I dared not confide my unlovedness with peers whose story lines, I believed, ran so perpendicularly to mine. Lest they laugh, I stuffed endless comparisons inside. In the company of a sympathetic listener, I feared unleashing dammed feelings would confirm my unworthiness and drive kindness away.

The kind-heartedness of Teacher *Trị*, our literature instructor, stirred up particularly poignant hope that I might summon up the courage to express myself. In her course, we were assigned group work which was novel in itself. Works of Vietnamese fiction of the 1920s and 30s were read and presented. As each panel guided the rest of the class through an author's style, plot, character development, metaphors, and more, our seated schoolmates could question us. Like a referee, *Trị* kept the always lively banter within bounds. We loved tussling over ideas and tried out rhetorical tricks to lead our audience into asking questions we could answer with ease in order to magnify our quite paltry expertise and boost our grades. Each participant received this teacher's evaluation and thoughtful criticism of our information, depth and methods. I discovered how much deeper learning was when I had to articulate it concisely and meaningfully to someone else.

The intersection of brevity and wit called poetry stumped me. Well-thumbed though my book of poems became, long-dead poets blazed too circuitous a route to meaning for me. My teacher instilled an appreciation of technique; I recognized the skill of these wizards of words but the array of interpretations struck me as utterly impractical. At fifteen, I found no pleasure in others' ambiguity. Though a closet dreamer myself, I couldn't catch the fringes of some visionary's magic carpet even if the view from above might have broadened my horizons over the mine-fields I was walking through below.

Wary of disclosing our weaknesses, most adolescent student peers and I remained relative strangers. After school hours, there was almost no socializing, no diversion from family duties, and certainly no safety in coming and going anywhere. In 1971, as the scale of combat increased, a handful were conscripted out of our class. A weightiness settled on our hearts. Great pressure to pass examinations or be called to die burdened the boys. Like them, I lived day to day, walking blindly into my future. On any given day, tripping off unexploded ordnance along the path to or from school might leave me limbless or lifeless. Where some people found tonic in the stress-relief of repetitive tasks like knitting, I preferred retreating to the silent cleft in my mind. There I tried to piece sense out of existence. Rather than fear, my foremost mood was hopelessness. At my bleakest, I despaired of effecting any change at all. Amplified by daily danger, the existence of evil could not be discounted. All the vileness I knew intensified my thirst for good.

"This life, what is it? Why is it?"

"How does this fate fall to that person?"

"What mires my people in such misery?"

"Which wrong accounts for constant sorrow?"

What contrast I saw between mangled earth and untouched sky! The wonderer in me couldn't reconcile brokenness and beauty.

Disrupting my incessant and private pondering were final exams. I was at a crossroads. Superior grades could assure me an opportunity to matriculate and enter university within a year. Achieving first-class standing could alternatively open an immediate way out of the precarious countryside and into the city if I were accepted as a student nurse. My application to the School of Nursing next door to South Vietnam's finest hospital, *Chợ Rẫy*, was one among more than a thousand. A month after sitting the four-hour entry examination, I received the tide-turning news. Along with forty-nine other young women, I should pack my bag and present myself to the authorities at *Cán Sự Điều Dưỡng* in September, 1972. And so I slipped out from under *Má's* chafing reproach at the futility of education, evading, as well, the anxiety and daily danger lurking in the provinces.

Εvery Scar a Badge of Beauty

Stopping in *Trần Hoàng Quân* Street, I stared up at the Residence for Nurses in Training of the National Nursing Board of South Vietnam. Would the institute make a nurse of me? I had never entered a hospital for care, let alone to care. I wasn't some smug smart-aleck upstart. Aspiring to best nobody, but to better myself, I had beaten the odds. On the basis of academic merit alone, these doors were swinging open before me. Ahead, book-learning would not be enough. Hand and eye coordination could not suffice. Fragile feelings would need to be steeled lest wobbly knees succumbed to fainting or a lonely heart mistook empathy for infatuation. None of this I suspected. A naïve and uneasy eighteen-year-old stood on the threshold of her transformation.

Through the laboratory of dormitory living, most of our class of fifty were launched immediately into new learning about human psychology. The bashfulness and giggles of unfamiliarity among young women rooming together soon wore off. A lower bunk in a wide room of thirty stacked beds was assigned to me. There I sat, labelling everything from pencils to panties. At home there had never been any question of which were mine. Aside from one drawer in the night table separating my bed from the next, I had a little locker in a string of metal cabinets to store clothing -one *áo dài*, two uniforms, mandatory cap, closed toe shoes - and weighty books: anatomy, pharmacology, pathology, English. We ate and drank those texts, and sometimes slept with them. The occasional thud in the night, more than likely a book that tumbled off an upper bunk, announced who had drifted off, studying under the covers. For although evening study hall ran from seven to nine o'clock, there was so much to read that the last hour before lights out found many of us poring over our books or quizzing each other. Whispers from corners after ten meant someone was still cramming, willing medical terminology into memory.

Our initial three months were foundational theory and rudimentary skills. Eight hours a day, Monday through Saturday, lectures and labs integrated lessons as we practiced procedures on placid mannequins and feistier peers. Taking blood pressure, making beds - both empty or occupied by helpful or helpless "patients", applying principles of body mechanics to lift safely and stretch - but not too far, our instructors demonstrated proper techniques before scrutinizing every oversight in our initial attempts. Their correction was firm yet for me fun; I reveled in the cohesion of intention and action.

Because the Department of Health was committed to international medical partnerships, our classes included English curriculum and preparation for personnel exchanges with Japanese hospitals. Our world widened and our knowledge deepened although some self-doubt lingered. I didn't truly know within myself that I could be a nurse. The bar was set very high.

From day one, *Cô Dung's* stern face spelled out the solemnity of our vocation and sanctity of the lives we handled. Not a single one of us felt affection from or for our Director of Nursing during the three years under her authority. Yet, later, as nurses dressing the wounds of patients of every stripe, her integrity would become our spine. We learned that, like double-bladed daggers, every duty had to be handled with caution. Careful and correct intervention was the only defense of our patients and ourselves. Through carelessness, we could be wounded by our own errors. Indoctrination no less, to keep minutely detailed, accurate charts and precise records of vital signs, was the Director's forte. Once, in Professional Ethics as she lectured, pacing the floor at the front of the classroom, she paused at the sight of a student who had nodded off. Teacher *Dung* set her notes on the lectern.

"*Chị Liễu.*"

Sister Lieu.

Startled, *Liễu* looked up.

"*Chị Liễu*. Repeat my last sentence to the class."

Silence. The whirling fan whooshed a paper off the podium. Not a twitch. Not a titter.

Our professionalism should never be found wanting. Nurses were to model impeccable competence at all times. As young women, decorum demanded we handle male patients with particular care. No romantic relationships would be tolerated. One misguided liaison could damage public perceptions. Florence Nightingales were still not quite tolerated by traditional Vietnamese who claimed single females belonged under the family roof where they wouldn't fall for anyone unfit or unfamiliar. Regardless of gender, self-restraint demanded no intimacy with anyone under our charge; personal emotions would only interfere with objective care.

We, starry-eyed ingenues, loathed these lectures. We were then oblivious to discretion's rich recompense and barely scraped through Teacher's tests, hoping only to pass. *Cô Dung* accepted our animosity. With utmost consistency, she was intentional with every word and action well-thought out, just as she expected us to relate thoughtfully to every patient, medical student or doctor on the wards. Soon, in the operating room or at a bedside, everything she taught resonated in our minds and proved true.

Strict codes of conduct for our first practicum were matched by rigorous rules about the uniforms we wore: neatly pressed whites with socks below the knee and polished shoes that required daily cleaning. The pride and reputation of the national nursing school were resting on our shoulders, we were told, when we were first sent out of the classroom to tour a public health centre.

I felt more than butterflies in my stomach that first day among, literally, the great unwashed. Around my starched and stiff whites, I saw germs everywhere: critically serious sickness; napalm-induced wheezing; unrelieved breathlessness; puffy, pale faces; distended bellies. No one then went to hospital for a cold or low-grade fever. They shuffled in as a last resort.

I hung my head and hid at the back of the pack as our cohort was introduced to the head nurse and staff. If this was the real world where I might work for the rest of my life, I had grave doubts. Were we going to cure these broken bodies, or would they linger, leaking life before our eyes? In their expressions, I sensed despair. My own soul, long battling to discover myself, shuddered that such as these would look to me for recovery. Combat ever closer to home unnerved us nurses in training just as it shook up Vietnamese society at large. More than healing, hope was what we, all aware of our mortality, were dying for. In the Medicine Unit, parasites and gastrointestinal bleeding preceded transfusions. Swollen, shiny feet and sallow faces tipped us off to cardiac complaints. And pain, unmitigated, how could I manage that?

I was no tourist on those wards. After we students were guided through a department, two rows of narrow metal cots, fifty or sixty in all, we had work to do. Our hands moved folding screens around each bed where doctors conducted exams, or procedures were done. Our feet hurried to supply cupboards to bring whatever our superiors ordered. From the nursing station half way down the unit, could the charge nurse read the symptoms of my inner conflict as well as she knew the signs of every malady? My mind had been disciplined to retain, order and produce information but what mattered now was mastery of emotion and I was floundering. How hard I had studied! For what? To fail to check the feelings of discomfort, revulsion and fright could, I feared, bounce me from the city back to the village. The new-found camaraderie in teamwork, the intricate mysteries of physiology, and the aura of respect drew me to the profession but my aversion to splurting bodily fluids, vacant eyes and gut-wrenching cries almost euthanized any ambition. Assuming a single day's observations mirrored the scope of all hospital assignments, I barely talked myself into day two.

She was only a year or so younger than I was, a leukemia patient whose care from head to toe was delegated to me. The macrocosmic chaos of the Medicine Unit blurred in the hours focused on one girl's personal hygiene and nutrition. While I cajoled her into eating or washed her weakened body, I learned of her family, hard-up farmers along the western frontier. She needed blood but got iron supplements. Perhaps I also required a transfusion. Baffled self-absorption, my ignorant response to misery, drained me of what anaemic pity my immature heart could muster. Over the days, my hands and head carried on and cared for the chronically ill. Familiarity eased fear. Yet when I stood at the door heading for the next rotation, I surveyed, without heartfelt empathy, those who might never recover. Had they any hope of recuperation? Where would they go?

Where would I go? Three days running in the ER, I passed out at the sight of patients brought in awash in their own blood.

"Is nursing an appropriate career for you?"

Cô Dung's question hung in the air as I stood, barely breathing, in her airless office.

"You haven't conquered yourself. You have allowed your feelings to sweep your feet right out from under you!"

The abyss of failure gaped before me. I pulled myself together.

"Would you please give me one last chance? You won't have to suspend me. If I faint again, I will withdraw myself."

The secret was in centering on anything but the blood. Cool as my stainless steel scissors slitting the sleeves off the next patient, a skinned and fractured motorcyclist, I focused centimetre by centimetre up his torso and dodged the impact of the whole, bloody mess. With each snip, I pressed in turn each toe deliberately into the sweaty soles of my shoes willing my blood pressure up my limbs and into my brain. A resolute backbone, not another's unlucky guts and gore, would define my future. A farmhand I was determined not to become. Vicarious shock never again caused me to black out.

Intensive Care took mindfulness to new heights. Our very thorough instructor drew us aside as we trainees arrived. Antibiotic use and intravenous drips, like all correctly-administered treatments, could equip us in nurturing health but nothing surpassed the importance of the sentient care-giver. She impressed upon us the constant risk of infection, the consequences of dehydration and the extreme pain our intended help could cause a burn victim. With us assisting, our instructor demonstrated expert dressing changes. One woman had deep tissue burns over eighty percent of her skin. For four days, we tenderly tended to her raw and fragile body. Saturday was our half-day on wards before a Sunday off when the level of care would be reduced. After giving an injection for pain, our team rapidly unwrapped and rewrapped her legs, then we dressed her torso, back first, then chest. I was supporting her body when suddenly she slumped to one side.

"Are you alright?" I whispered by her bandaged ear.

But she was gone.

One moment, the young woman was the object of every ounce of our compassion, the next instant, the subject of a great grief. For every soul who strives to alleviate suffering and elevate life, the first death is an acute loss. She was mine. All the good-will that had motivated us to go the extra mile for her was shattered. The weight of mortality bore down on me. Had we killed her with kindness? What if we hadn't done that dressing? Would she have lived?

At each phase of my training, I experienced sensitivities unlike the previous. The third of my practical placements was Maternity where all idyllic illusions of motherhood withered. My overwhelming first impression on wending my way through the overflowing waiting room was noise. Heaving sighs and pitched voices shrilled through cubicle curtains. There was a surfeit of unrestrained emotion.

"'No,' I had told you. 'Enough.' But no, oh no, no, no, you just kept right on coming. You dog! You animal! Look at me now. An instant of pleasure, hours of pain. And you think you're going to walk on out leaving me to face this alone? Deserter!"

I heard no word from the apparent father and saw some silent ladies bite their lips. Another loud mouth woman shrieked at the first.

"You'd've been better off keeping your mouth and your legs shut! You wouldn't be here if you knew how to keep your thighs together!"

Overhearing such unmentionable things, we young ladies in white turned redder than ripe beets. Sexual intimacy had never been broached in conversation in our homes; lectures in human reproduction by unblushing professors were all about the systems, never touching the part of passion. How many in that room did reckless indiscretion account for? What kind of world was this? Labour lived up to its name.

In the Delivery Room, my first observation assignment was made easier by an almost textbook case. I had barely recovered my equilibrium when a breech birth presented. Seizing the small, slippery buttocks, the physician braced his foot against the table and twisted the tiny protruding hips. His vigorous wrenching would snap the baby's neck, I was sure. In my horror, I imagined his hands fishing out the skull after a discombobulated body cleared the birth canal. But no, the doctor persisted in the procedure, perspiration plastering his skull cap and greens to his own body, until the head emerged. My classmate and I, apprehensive and amazed, gazed at the florid-faced infant while his lungs were suctioned. An attending nurse swatted him hard on the behind.

"You're a stubborn one! Cry! Cry!"

When cry he did, I simply shut down emotionally.

How cruel the end of life could be I had recently witnessed, but at that birth I collided with the harshness of our entrance into this world. All my questions about human frailty multiplied; all answers evaporated.

Philosophy class treated being, substance and essence in an exceedingly clinical way. With new clarity I saw how insufficient my definition of knowing had been. In my noticing, recognizing and identifying the human condition, I had been focusing only on the sun-dappled waves of a great, dark, unimagined deep. Time and space and chance were inadequate to account for the layered pangs of childbirth, the exponential growth of fused egg and sperm bursting out in death-defying frenzy. I craved cause.

Like a little one just ripped from the womb without prior knowledge of good or evil, I seemed newborn, experiencing hurt, filth and ruptured bonds as never before. All pain's ugliness left me queasy. How blind I had been to the sorrow or spite behind every penciled brow, lipsticked smile or well-cut suit in Saigon's streets. Naked, humanity shuddered at the shadow we cast upon the beauty of the Earth. No wardrobe and no words could adequately cover our scars, although we tried. In the dormitory, after lights-out, I brooded but didn't ask the other girls why no one chitchatted that night.

Come morning, I paused at the infants' bassinets and wondered at another face of birth. Utterly beautiful babies, black-fringed faces and dark-eyed, cooed or slumbered. Delicate lips pursed and pulsed as mothers, delivery disregarded, gently placed tiny mouths to breast. This scene was a universe away from the previous day's pain. For the first time in my life, I observed in a mother's eyes, immeasurable love for her child. Her palpable joy transfixed me.

Yet I could not linger. My services were required for post-op mothers. Caesarian-section patients presented the nastiest chores of nursing, post-partum care. Some women knew how to care for their bodies but others lacked the know-how to keep clean and uncontaminated. At the stench of discharge, disheveled bodies and soiled linens, it was a wonder that I didn't add my own vomit to the revolting scene. On one filthy mattress lay the rude-mouthed woman from the day before. I confess she was particularly loathsome to me; dispassionate I was not.

Zeal for presentability wasn't enough to get through a shift tidily over the next two weeks. Back in Delivery, I caught the excitement of catching babies. Amid amniotic fluid, excrement and blood, I concentrated on the crowning head rather than my splattered shoes and socks. Those would have to wait for bleach and polish. Tolerating the hullabaloo of hollered curses, screeching moans and constant coaching often bellowed above the commotion, I exhaled long and low, released from urgency's clutch at each emerging infant's gasping "ei-yeiiii!" Tiny tongues quivered as little lungs finally filled with the breath of life.

On the Surgical floor, I refined my instinctive response - a sharp, involuntary intake of air - at the sight of amputees, bullet-pocked bodies, the war wounded. The ordnance somebody's mommy or daddy assembled nine to five in some peace-loving American town was blowing off Vietnamese feet, imbedding facefuls of shrapnel, and shredding flesh and bone from the *Bến Hải* River to the Mekong Delta. Sterilizing, soothing, setting, sealing gashes. Fractures, lesions, lacerations, these were the trenches of my trembling hands. Sepsis was the enemy within. Every scar was a badge of beauty, a victorious line of defiance in the teeth of death.

Life out of uniform began at noon on Saturdays, a thirty-six hour reprieve from the rigid weekday routine of eight to five. Normally a two hour window was ours to do any errands or pursue personal pastimes. At seven in the evening our dormitory was locked. Males were not permitted past the entrance, the rendez-vous point for young ladies and admirers. Boyfriended or just generally cheeky classmates ran a risk by sneaking out afterwards and relying on those of us inside to unlatch doors or windows. Random rounds by the resident instructor weren't rigorous but if absence was noted, an offending student nurse would be called on the carpet. Many a weekend I escaped the Institute's antiseptic conventions to spend time with my sister's growing family. *Búp* had broken with tradition by finding her own husband, an American. They had three pint-sized darlings by the time

Hanhtiet [R], 1974, Nursing School

I moved to the capital city. From the second-storey balcony, Dan stretched up to the rail and Frank squinted through the bars, on auntie watch.

"She's coming! She's coming!"

The household help, *Dì Hai*, was dispatched to the main floor to let me in. After dinner, Dan would climb and cling on me. His arms cinched around my waist as he perched on the back of the bicycle while we whizzed up and down the street. When I had to leave, Dan's big hazel eyes easily welled with tears that sparkled in his long lashes and trickled down his cheeks. No sniffles from tough, tiny Frank. His hoarse little whisper and quick feet did or said whatever I asked.

Once, when the little ones were asleep, *Dì Hai*, twice my age, coaxed me out on the town to watch a dramatic performance called *cải lương*. Auntie, as I respectfully called *Dì Hai*, was a simple up-country peasant. The children loved her and *Búp* appreciated her help. My acceptance of *Dì Hai* as an equal regardless of her station in life cemented our relationship. She was utterly sincere, and transparent to a fault, with a love for Vietnamese traditional opera she could rarely indulge; the theatre wasn't a place for an unescorted woman. That night the familiar theme of dastardly mother-in-law mistreating defenceless daughter-in-law wound into a tighter and tauter pitch. As the crescendo to climax careened to the rafters, Auntie drew her feet up under her on the seat. Her muscles tensed like a tigress about to spring. Wholly one with the action, *Dì Hai* hurled one flip-flop on stage, mercifully hitting no one. She shrieked, cursing the matronly actress for feint more real than reality.

"You'd better move on out. So brutal. So cruel. May lightning strike you dead!"

At Auntie's curses, I shrank mortified into my seat, then reached up and yanked her back into her own. My shushing and reprimands yielded no good. The orchestral fervour foreshadowed impending doom and *Dì Hai's* second shoe spun through the air this time thwacking a patron on the head. Apologies ensued as the audience groused about distractions from the show they had actually paid to see.

My humiliation ebbed as we tripped home in the dark, Auntie griping about the gravel grinding her shoeless soles.

"Next time," I paused to compose myself, "Next time you go to the theatre, take a sackful of flipflops."

Irony went clear over *Dì Hai's* head.

"That woman had no right to abuse the young lady. No right!"

"Those actors didn't really strike each other, Auntie. Their slapstick antics are what we paid for. Perhaps their art is too compelling for you. If you make a spectacle of yourself, I won't go with you again." *Cải lương*, comic or tragic, was a rare diversion for me.

Half way through nurses training, I petitioned our administration for permission to write the national baccalaureate examinations. Hand-written since their inception, a multiple choice cum-card alternative was introduced in 1974. Over two dozen keeners in our class who, like me, had foregone university entrance to study nursing, and three instructors who had done the same years before, wanted to challenge the grade twelve compulsory subjects. Biology and chemistry were not unrelated to our field. Preparing for geography, history, mathematics, physics, Vietnamese literature and the English or French language exams added a lot to our already full plates. I put my money where my mouth was and paid the examination fees. The Board of Nursing hesitated, then consented. Their faith in us was rewarded.

The following year at our graduation, *Cô Dung's* formidable command finally relaxed. Her mission complete, a gratified smile transformed her into the openhearted mentor to whom many of us would turn as we launched our careers. An hour after convocation, we graduates entered a lock-up to await placement by the Department of Health. As government-trained nurses, we automatically became civil servants to be dispatched to hospitals and health centres according to need. A key rattled in the door and a health official strode in, a wax-sealed envelope in her hand. She explained the procedure. The seal would be broken; she would display the list of all South Vietnamese hospitals detailing where nurses were required. The student with the top marks would begin the process, selecting any posting she wished. Jostling to see the job prospects, we couldn't breathe. This was wartime but being in the city had shielded us from the worst of it. What if we were posted to the front-lines? There were only three employment opportunities in Saigon, so few for a class of fifty. I stood sixth in the class. Our valedictorian chose the hospital just north of the capital in *Bình Dương*. The second also opted to be close to family in *Biên Hòa City*. When the third spoke for her home town in *Bình Dương* too, I pressed my lips together to stifle the cheer surging up in me. Staying in Saigon meant *Má's* hold would wane while career opportunities waxed brighter. Student Four selected the pediatrics post at the *Bệnh Viện Nhi Đồng* facility, then Five took the opening at the orthopedics institute. Employment at *Chợ Rẫy* was mine! This was Vietnam's largest hospital and the only one in the south with a neurological surgery department. Letters were sent from the Board of Nursing introducing each nurse to her new employer.

Tết was approaching as we emptied our lockers and bundled up belongings and memories of three years together. Many girls stretched out their leave over the New Year celebrations. I, however, wanted to avoid combat with *Má* and informed her I had to work. At twenty-one, I had studied a decade longer than Ma's limit. She had been hankering after a share of my earning power since I had finished fifth grade. This time I met with no objections to cutting short my visit home.

All In

In February 1975, I reported for my first shift. *Chợ Rẫy's* eleven floors, recently re-equipped with Japanese assistance, dominated District 5 of Saigon, which we Vietnamese knew as *Cholon*. Vendors in a once vast vegetable bazaar, who had been displaced to make room for the hospital expansion, now spread throughout the Chinese quarter. The administrative division of the hospital opened my file with sheaves of forms and payroll documents. The vacancy was in Emergency. Was I aware that my probationary period pay would be reserved until I had successfully completed three months? Yes. Would I sign on immediately? I signed.

Rather than rent a bed in the staff residence, I took *Búp* and George up on the offer of the apartment they had first bought for just the two of them. It was only a ten minute bicycle ride from the hospital. As I rode, I wanted to holler "I am free!" Along the road to independence, I had negotiated many twists with good results. Sharp corners and abrupt breaks hadn't toppled me. I sensed the confidence of cresting a new height. Had *Bà Ngoại* primed me for the pace and responsibility of being entirely on my own? Constraining my liberty was some unease at my want of wise counsel. Decision-making without elders was onerous for one such as I.

The latest in medical machinery, built in and brought from Japan, made *Chợ Rẫy* a modern, high-tech marvel compared to other hospitals. The end of one learning was the beginning of another. Guerneys and beds rolled, lifted and lowered effortlessly. Oxygen tele-posts accommodated various procedural configurations. My seniors tutored me in intubating; I became proficient at suturing skin tears, inserting IVs and drawing blood samples. *Cô Dung's* hard line on hygiene served me well as cutting edge equipment was nothing without sterile technique.

Snapping on another pair of stretchy yellow latex gloves as each new case was assessed, the whizzing pace of the ER grew on me. There was order in the automaticity of meticulous protocol; like a limber parasympathetic system, our nursing team heard orders and enacted them. Senior staff engaged newer grads at every step. Precision and efficiency by design stimulated my mind while encasing every movement in a serenity I could not have imagined weeks earlier.

A young girl, belly full of herbicide, was my first case of attempted suicide. Within minutes of her arrival, the poison was identified and she was stabilized on the way to treatment. Ashen-faced parents who wouldn't stand for forbidden love now wrung their hands while we pumped toxic stomach contents. Another venom flowed in the veins of a Montagnard, one of many viper bite victims from the highlands. Around the puncture wound, his skin distended and discoloured. The semi-conscious patient laboured to breathe under our monitoring. As if a krait still lurked, I sensed a serpentine constriction around my own heart. My autonomic response to snakes of all shapes and sizes had always been vocal histrionics and paralysis of the legs. There was no time or place for side-stepping duty. We were on to an ectopic pregnancy. Death was imminent; would the stalker take one or both? Inevitably during the three to eleven shift, one or more inebriated motorcyclists would stagger, or be lugged, through the door. Helmetless, wretched and retching, the many head-trauma cases always came to *Chợ Rẫy* for its unique neurology care. In those days, other brain injuries such as strokes usually arrived comatose, long past early intervention opportunities to minimize damage. Lack of oxygen, particularly cases of severe asthma, initially scared me stiff. Remarkably, immediate and critical care in cases of cardiac arrest was seldom needed. The aged, almost always somewhat mobile and rarely over-round, tended to pass suddenly at home, or along a lane. It was commonly said that an evil wind had invaded their body and snatched their breath away. I was not an instinctual first-responder, but once I learned to read the signs, my head and hands aligned.

My heart, I happily realized in those early months, was in it too. I lapped up every learning opportunity. When co-workers with far-flung families wanted to trade shifts for extra days off, I was always amenable. Our rotations were a day, two evenings, and a night followed by twenty-four hours rest. As a hungry probationary employee, I filled up on cafeteria lunch, dinner or breakfast. Although I was rarely off my feet for thirty minutes over eight hours, the end of shift would find me lingering with post-op patients. Following up was very fulfilling. Every resuscitation and every individual resting in recovery was reward enough for the earlier tension and uncertainty. Whether I was out of my scrubs at mid-afternoon, just past sunrise, or after peak afternoon and evening hours, the life and death worth of our work invigorated me. It was very satisfying to be accepted on a skillful team that delivered the highest level of care.

To be welcomed, every free evening, with eager hugs and fervent kisses of the sweet children I cherished topped off those days. Free to come or go as I pleased, I liked nothing better than burrowing into the sense of family that *Búp* and George's home extended to me. I belonged. I basked in my sister's pleasure at my success. My nephews and new niece begged for time with auntie. I obliged Dan with overnight sleeps at my apartment although he seemed even more attached to *Bà Giáo*, the grandmotherly tenant one floor above, than to me. The prolonged conversations between these five and seventy-five-year-olds intrigued me. Many a penny paperback lay unread in my lap when curiosity at cross-generational giggles, whys, and ahahs overcame me.

Silence spoke volumes too, especially concerning my diminutive niece. If she were out of sight and soundless, something was up. We might find her, oh so still, shredding tissues into ever more infinitesimal pieces. Once, all our calling exhausted, I noticed, above wriggling toes, Josie's panty-clad little body squeezed inside the *Thần Tài*, or money-god household shrine, in *Búp's* living room. Joss-sticks, mangosteen and water goblet, offered for future fortune, lay evicted on the floor tiles.

Whatever household task was at hand, middle-child Frank was my shadow.

"What are you doing? I can help!"

His help often meant more, not less, needed doing. The end of the matter was predictable.

With characteristic contemplation, he would solemnly shake his head, bright eyes fixed on mine, and conclude, "It is TOO hard. I can't do it."

Too much for me was even a whiff of the personal pillow my nephew preferred to sleep on. Whenever I laundered it, the scent of soap affronted Frank. Weeping and gnashing of teeth ensued. How he could be so attached to a casing full of feathers was beyond me.

On my days off, all three kids camped out at my place. They napped through the muggiest tropical afternoons splayed on somewhat cooler tile floors, each in a corner. Tiny Josie fell asleep fast. Frank, if far enough from siblings' poking fingers or prodding tongue, snuggled close to me and soon rolled over in a gentle snore. Dan, still nursing a soother, lay on his back one foot slowly rocking, rocking. Behind the sweep of his luxurious eyelashes, I couldn't tell if sleep had come. When the time came for kindergarten, that pacifier became an issue.

"I'm SO proud of you. You're a big boy going to school and all. Soothers, you know, are for babies."

I waited. Dan deliberated.

"Should we throw it away?"

"Away? If I put it in the trash, will I be your big boy?"

"I'd say you already are my big boy."

Dan trotted over to the fridge where he liked the soother to chill. Took it out. Crossed the floor to the waste bin. Glanced down at the rubber nipple in his chubby hand. Turned wonderingly up at me. Down. Up. Again. Again. His hand placed the soother in the garbage and he never looked back. Many a spin around the neighbourhood on my bicycle rewarded Dan's resolve.

Not all wheels turned with such equilibrium. *Búp* was learning to drive, or rather, George was paying a driving school to get his wife past grinding the gears, to be able to ferry their family around the city herself. One day she asked me to watch the kids.

I assumed 'I'll practice' meant going out and driving. But the car stayed inside the gated yard while *Búp* sat in the driver's seat revving the engine from time to time.

"Where did you go?" I queried when my sister rejoined us in the house.

"Nowhere."

A recollection of my own chagrin at bungled attempts on a bicycle stirred sympathy.

"Is that all the teacher taught you?"

"I'm scared."

Since dodging the hurly-burly of Saigon traffic was too much for *Búp* behind the wheel, she and the children joined me on a diesel-belching bus to *Biên Hòa*. My satchel was stocked with medication for *Bà Ngoại's* stomach ailment, cough syrup, and city remedies for country folk. In my mind's eye, once my unpaid three-month internship was complete, I would buy from bolts I'd been fingering in the fabric market, have a tailor fashion new clothes, bring money, and replace Grandmother's tatty sweater. I imagined that participation in the medical personnel exchange arranged between *Chợ Rẫy* and Japan held promise of even greater rewards to come. In *Bà Ngoại's* orchard, Dan and I filched fruit with impunity. For, despite my best efforts to tutor him in the stealth I'd sharpened at his age, Dan's exuberant, "That one! I like that one!" was never rebuked by *Bà Ngoại*. Perhaps great-grandmother status had softened her. Among the trunks and boughs of trees grown fruitful under my care, she would let us know she knew what we were up to. Wordlessly permission was granted. By the time goodbyes were said and the ferry was carrying us away from the coconut palms and bamboo thickets, the island's peace had settled upon my heart. Without rapids or ripples, the *Đồng Nai* River flowed in my blood. That I could be untroubled was another wonder. My world was about to undergo a seismic shift.

This Was That

My sister's whispers that she might have to go with her children and their father to his country was the first tremor rattling my most treasured relationships. In my naiveté, war was a constant, North and South Vietnam having been in conflict all of my life. No province was untouched by bloodletting, no family inviolate. Even so, the violence was not of my making and I did not take up arms any more than I joined the perpetual spat between my mother and grandmother. However, in early 1975, the fault line that ran through our family began to gape. Within three months the chasm would split us irretrievably apart. I didn't see it coming.

Our ER continued to serve civilians caught between combatants although Saigon itself had been spared direct hits since before I had arrived as a student. Hospital administrators created emergency response teams to relocate medical care should rocket bombardment befall us. The evacuation drills may have given men in cuff-links and cravats a sense of preparedness but no amount of simulation could compensate for unrealistic expectations.

Huế, our ancient capital, fell to the *Việt Cộng*. The south tensed as the embattled central provinces were lost. News was bad, rumour dire. We heard but did not understand. We saw but did not perceive. *ĐàNẵng* and *Đàlạt* were taken. *Nha Trang* was overcome. Extreme anxiety flooded Saigon along with masses of civilians fleeing ahead of the troops who were retreating from the provinces toward the city.

George told *Búp* little. I knew even less. Ignorance was not bliss. In mid-April, my sister urged me to wheedle my way out of work for a few days to move all her household furnishings to my apartment. She had been to the bank. Six hundred thousand piasters in fresh, crisp cash passed from her hand into mine. This was surreal. Laughing in disbelief, I fingered the new bills unstained by tobacco, grease or fish sauce. Intense emotions lurked behind surprise. What to do? I understood then that my brother-in-law was deliberate and inflexible regarding his family's future. I sensed an invisible winch winding the bond between us, stretching it to the limit, drawing my niece, nephews and sister up and away, far, far away from me. This impending personal loss eclipsed the looming national surrender. Indeed, I did not see that the country would be lost. No analysis of the causes of the American war or the consequences of the hasty withdrawal crossed my mind. All Vietnamese were the same, I simplistically supposed. One regime would be like another.

On orders from her husband, *Búp* and the children stopped going out. Anywhere. I hurried over after work. Turning off the thoroughfare, looking up their lane, whenever I spied the kids on the balcony, I sighed relief. If they were out of view, my pulse pounded as I ran up the steps. Would they just vanish? One day, they did.

"*Búp?* Are you here?"

I felt as though I'd tripped into an abyss and was falling, tumbling, dropping down, down, down. The house echoed. Hollow-hearted, I retrieved *Búp's* handwritten note in agreed-upon code.

"We're leaving to visit the children's grandparents."

There was more, of course, but that was all I learned that awful Friday that emptied my life of loving ones. I sat sobbing.

"Where are you?"

Artillery fire could be heard from *Tân Sơn Nhất* airport. My only hope was that they had already flown out of harm's way.

Alone and lonely, I slept on my sister's sofa crowded into my room along with her dining table and chairs. The ounces of gold I'd bought with *Búp's* wad of cash were cold comfort. I sewed these beneath a false bottom in the shoulder bag that carried my soiled or laundered uniforms. Outside the apartment block, the city was unraveling into chaos. I heard intermittent shelling; inside the bachelor's suite, only the ticking of the clock. Loneliness lived with me. Just after dawn, I made my way through uneasy streets to *Chợ Rẫy* for my scheduled day shift. Later the hospital public address system crackled to life with the numbing news of capitulation. President General *Dương Văn Minh*, in power for only a few days, had given up what he didn't have. It was the thirtieth of April, *"Ngày Mất Nước"*, the day we southerners lost our country.

Across the Emergency Room, doctors, nurses, orderlies, clerks, ambulance attendants and patients stared at each other, dazed and disoriented. Unbelievable. It felt like someone had swung a massive hammer concussing skulls and leaving us seeing stars. Trauma cases began pouring through the doors. The less wounded delivered graver cases into our care. Gunshots everywhere left many dead. Republican uniforms were shed by South Vietnamese soldiers who hadn't succumbed to self-inflicted bullets or shots from northern fighters or southern communists now showing their true colours. All order disintegrated. Enemies lay side by side filling every bed, every stretcher, covering the floor and spilling into the ambulance bay. I moved among the injured, tiptoeing around and between bodies, squatting down to attend to one while the next tugged at my sleeve and another took his last breath.

Rather than heading out into anarchy, I stayed on through the afternoon and evening. Three days later, I realized I couldn't remain in the hospital forever. Fearful that everyone in any uniform might be considered a collaborator with the Americans, I began pulling on my street clothes. A colleague counseled me that professional dress would mark me as a professional and ensure some respect. I dithered, eyeing vermilion splotches on my socks, sangria-like splatter from collar to cuff. My scrubs hardly looked respectable. Seventy-some hours endlessly touching bloodied, limbless, moaning casualties and I was falling apart. Like a few droplets of soap in an ocean of atrocity, my efforts at relief seemed squandered. I found my bicycle intact, and careened up the street, cycling like a maniac.

Hundreds of operating rooms in simultaneous surgery couldn't have kept pace with the fallout from surrender. Despite official cessation of hostilities, medical services were strained to the brink for a further two weeks. To get us to our now sixteen-hour-long shifts, an ambulance collected *Chợ Rẫy* staff from home. Within a week of celebrating victory, proclaiming the grand reunification of Vietnam, *Việt Cộng* assumed control of the hospital. Our long-serving and long-suffering chief of staff had always maintained integrity in adhering to professional standards of hospital administration. He had no option but to put up with a theatrical transfer of authority ceremony. Then he disappeared.

More Northerners appeared among us, ostensibly to teach us how to do our own jobs. Abysmal medical knowledge and ignorance of cutting-edge equipment seemed directly correlated to rank. The sketchier the skill, the grander the political pull. We Southerners were suspect. Our techniques and treatments were disregarded. Our intolerable contempt had to be checked. We were to listen. We were to do as told. Morale plummeted. Mortality mounted.

My dreams were dust. My employment probationary period passed but compensation never came. Payroll had no piasters for service past. I would never be paid for those first three months. Norms of work and life, financial obligations and social contracts spun out of control. With priority care now mandated for villagers long cut off from urban health centres, our Emergency Department was admitting hundreds more patients every twenty-four hours. The flood of assessments was channeled to appropriate units or other city hospitals specializing in pediatrics or orthopedics. Other patients were monitored around the clock and discharged symptomless. Severe malaria cases spiked as fevered jungle warriors brought the parasitic malaise into the city. Intermittently abnormal or fluctuating temperatures with intense shakes and violent vomiting threatened the lives of many. Over time, their livers, red blood cells and entire circulatory systems surrendered.

Hearts were giving way to what we came to name "the modern condition". Suicide, long the rare and reckless act of pregnant girls abandoned by reprobate lovers, shifted demographics. Around *Chợ Rẫy, Cholon's* Chinese community, which had seldom been ostentatious with the wealth generations had accumulated, became easy prey when the Sino-Vietnamese socialist brotherhood broke down. Confucian virtues were toppled by the seizure of private assets and recalibrating of currency. In lieu of banks, all closed, the new regime set up exchanges where already-almost-useless piasters were to be handed in for *đồng.* Without advance notice, amplifiers blaring from trucks broadcast a three hour window to swap old notes for new legal tender. Already distrustful, I registered very little of *Búp's* stash, and received in return the maximum three hundred new bills everyone was calling *Bác Hồ,* Uncle *Hồ.* Six years after his death, *Hồ Chí Minh* was in everyone's pocket. Over the next three years, revaluations recurred, each time further impoverishing holders of paper funds.

The wiser wealthy held gold. Night-time police sweeps through the district rattled importers, grocers, tailors, restauranteurs and their families. Pressure tactics ferreted out ingeniously hidden bullion; for instance, after hauling alleged capitalists out of bed and into the street, sharp-eyed accusers followed furtive glances. A lingering look at chunky chains cinching house plant pots to balcony rails was a dead giveaway; officers flaked off tinted coatings to reveal the precious metal.

Many entrepreneurs, small business-men mostly, lost every means to honour their ancestors, provide for their descendants, and ultimately to face the world. Self-administered poisoning seemed the most expedient exit from such disgrace. They arrived at the hospital in the arms of grieving loved ones, on trishaws, in taxis or cars, and handcuffed in paddy wagons. The ignominy of failed suicide afflicted patients whose stomachs we pumped, whose comas we monitored, whose systems were cleansed. Some regained consciousness only to beg me to assist in ending the indignity of life. Their despair haunted me. I stroked silky, unhardened hands, some still ringed in diamonds, and massaged uncalloused feet. Chinese names on charts at heads of beds matched bruised bodies. When contusions couldn't have been self-inflicted, had police brutality exacted secrets? Intrusive sentries demanded explanations of every medical procedure. Once open, listless eyes lighting on police guards filled with fear. Words could not tell more poignantly of despondency. If stabilized, these patients were escorted out to police cars that whisked them away, likely not for better but for worse. Would there have been more mercy in complicity with their requests for medically assisted death? Poise, self-possession, and dignity had already died. Assisting rather than resisting death was a slur upon all living, was it not? Hippocratic ethics spurred formation of a specialized team to handle the stream of single suicides and even entire families whose poison-laced last suppers miscarried. Doubt ate away at me. We were a society in disarray. Unsteady minds and souls found no peace in death and no rest in sleep.

After an entire shift on my feet, I went home and took off my false, impassive face. I disclosed my mounting apprehension to the photos of *Búp* and her children that filled every frame in my room. No one sat in their chairs. No one could fill their places. Were they living or had they died? I sighed, murmured condolences to myself, and wept. Eventually I slept. I woke for work and left, locked inside myself.

Uncle *Hai* came calling. *Má's* older brother had eight mouths to feed and bare cupboards. Surely a niece on the hospital payroll could share. No? Nobody believed anybody. A few weeks later, he showed up at the ambulance entrance. Neither he nor any of his six grown children had work. Could I spare a little rice or extend a loan? At that point I had forty-seven *đồng* – enough for two weeks' worth of breakfasts – and no patience.

"Do not ask me again. From now on, all I can provide are medications for *Bà Ngoại*. When I can get them, I'll drop them off at your home so someone can take them out to *Biên Hòa*. Do not come here again."

But I didn't trust him. I never left anything saleable in his hands. I finagled the forty-five kilometre ride out to the island and took my 80 year-old grandmother her meds myself. *Má* wasn't eating or sleeping. Anxious, she turned to me, her loyal daughter. Word was out that *Má's* traitorous eldest had accompanied her husband to villain America.

"Your daughter went with our enemy" was what wagging tongues were repeating in haughty tones.

Villagers weren't necessarily neighbourly at the best of times and this was not that. I felt ambushed by unrelenting family requests and cornered by escalating fear.

Toward the end of June, the local authorities in District 3 of Saigon, now officially renamed *Hồ Chí Minh* City, rapped on my door. They claimed to be taking inventory of whatever I had inside.

"Ridiculous!"

I refused them entry. "This room is not some villa!"

Later three men and a woman knocked.

"This apartment is owned by your sister, not you."

They accused me of squatting and ordered me to leave; the men were moving in. I unlatched the security chain and opened the door, railing at them. They stepped back, ominously threatening to return. A couple of weeks later, I arrived home to find the lock damaged. The same three thugs were inside. Every drawer, cupboard and box had been rummaged through.

I knew then that I was going to lose all my possessions. There were weapons in their hands and absurd aims in their minds. If they pointed at a cat and said, 'It's a chicken,' one was to say, 'It's a chicken.' I let them have a piece of my mind.

"This is my home. You are not allowed. Get out!"

"We are here on the orders of Comrade So and So."

"I don't care! Tell your Mister So and So to be here tomorrow at this time. We will talk then. Out!"

My fury had not subsided the next day; I understood I no longer had a home. Inventory had been taken and all my earthly goods confiscated. I demanded that the cadre add a declaration to the list of household wares.

"Against my will, I, an employee of the government, have been removed from my home and deprived of the following possessions..."

He wrote my words and signed the meaningless document in an impervious, precise hand. My hands were empty, my ire spent. I left with the clothes on my back. Although I had been born into poverty, I had never before been without a roof over my head. As a helpless child dependent on my widowed grandmother, I had always had a place to sleep. Now, newly capable of supporting myself independently, I was absolutely destitute.

My white-knuckled fingers clutched the bicycle grips as I pedaled blindly up the street. Tears coursed down my cheeks; hysteria seized me. Where could I turn?

Compassionate colleagues, seven nurses taking turns on five cots in the hospital staff residence, made room for me. We shared a toilet and shower, and one closet for our street clothes with pegs on the walls to hang uniforms. The fan ran twenty-four seven, never quite cooling those fifteen square metres where off-shift workers slept, and privacy was reduced to closing one's eyes. We hoarded cardboard boxes when unpacking medical supplies. Since we couldn't afford charcoal or wood for our tiny clay brazier, burning cartons cooked our rice.

Once a month, we each received vouchers for 500 grams of unrefined sugar. On the booming black market, I sold my sweetener at three or four times the official price. Haggling, always standard market procedure, became an art as I traded up my ration of canned condensed milk and fatty back bacon. The hospital canteen was the source of thirteen kilos of deplorable raw rice, gritty with sand or even going moldy. Some months a blend of barley and rice, under a Soviet label, was distributed. At first everyone boiled it like pure rice and suffered the consequences of constipation, colon problems and hemorrhoids. When sacks of ground wheat were substituted, I was baffled. No one had access to an oven. I had never cooked with such powdery flour before. Noodle sellers were swamped with customers trying to exchange it for ready-to-boil pasta.

Hungry people were easily manipulated. For a slab of meat, a friend might turn informant. Back-stabbers could be bought with small but precious foodstuffs. 'Smile on the face, blade in the heart' was a maxim we the wary lived by. Kids were recruited to rat out their parents. Wives, primary or secondary, already suspected their husbands' scruples; men, in turn, had qualms about the reliability of the women they had wed or loved. Former officials or officers of the southern republic wound up in "re-education" – unending days of harsh agricultural labour followed by nights of self-criticism and political indoctrination – all in remote locations without even the basic necessities of life. The denunciations and accusations that led to missing parents also estranged traditional extended families. Love did not conquer all. Many engagements broke under ruthless rumours. Pledging one's troth appeared rash when truth was relative. A fiancé who disappeared might never return. Dead, serving decades-long sentences, or escaped, lovers left behind tattered promises. Too preoccupied with survival to even fantasize about romance, young people such as myself veered away from marriage vows. Might an attractive would-be intimate actually be an enemy? Cynicism achieved complete occupation of the mind. 'No faith had we in prince or peer' enshrined suspicion even in socialism's hymn, "L' Internationale".

Scrutiny of every aspect of life included laying bare one's personal history. As ordered by authorities, I listed all my family relationships including my half-sister, her whereabouts perhaps the United States of America.

"Can you come to my office?" was not an invitation to a consultation.

Once the door was closed, I heard for the first but hardly the last time an insanely unoriginal accusation.

"C. I. A."

I struggled to unscramble that then unfamiliar acronym, evidently a coded message. By the end of that first hours-long interrogation, I understood the allegation against me was espionage. Question upon question dizzied me; I felt like an insect swung by its antennae. Not a hair on my body had been touched but the assault on my mind depleted my nerve. What more could I say the next time I was seated behind that door? Repeated questioning drummed indecision into my brain. How had I answered each query in its last iteration? Uncertainty in answering confirmed my own misgivings about my ability to endure.

Grilled again and again, I began to question everyone else. Making any decision was torture. *Bà Ngoại* needed the medicine I'd squirreled away for her. But how should I get it to her? If I traded my canteen meal tins for bus fare to her village, I couldn't afford to eat until next month's allotment. Everywhere there were eyes, eyes, eyes. Peckish eyes noticed how much I had on my plate and made assumptions about what was in my pocket. Accusations and criticism bred easily in misery. How like animals we had become, snarling at anyone too close to the only bone we had to gnaw.

Yet unlike unreflective beasts, wistful people with imagination and initiative aspired to better. Innuendo linked unexplained disappearances not only to arrests but more and more to artful exits. I believed already that I had nothing left to lose. I began to believe that a reprieve from homelessness and hopelessness might actually exist ... elsewhere. Yet how could I find a way out? I heard of people making a break for freedom by sea, literally leaving their cloaks in the clutches of coast-guarding authorities. But, as I was without money, contacts, know-how, or trust, belief that I myself could run ran thin.

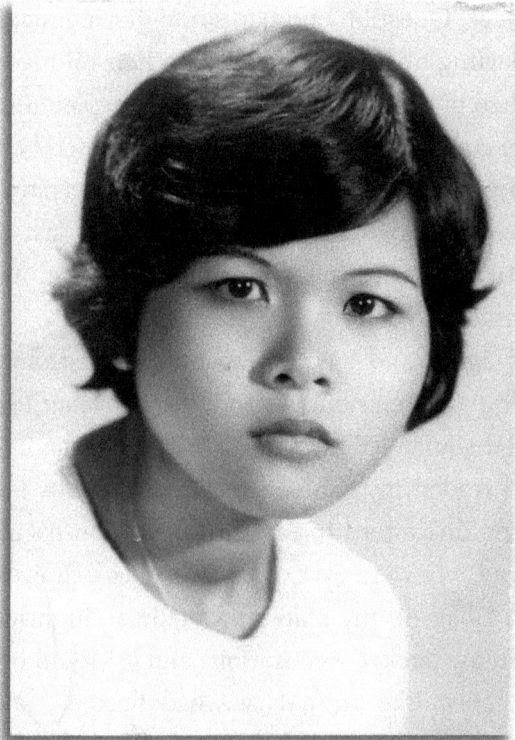

Hanhtiet, 1977, Hồ Chí Minh City

Shallow Hold

Two years into Vietnam's reunification, thoughts of flight, not food, consumed me. Back in April 1975, I had twice refused an out offered by a coworker whose relative, a high-ranking naval officer, had access to ships just off-shore, part of Operation Frequent Wind. Time had stopped when she stood in my doorway. A waiting port-bound engine rumbled in the street below. But *Má* and Grandmother's dependence rooted me to where I was. Love of the land reverberated in my heart. I had let safe passage go, so green was I in the field of regime change. Yet it was not only youthful hope that kept me there. Many older, should-have-been-wiser Vietnamese paid dearly for the ensuing lessons in compatriotic ill will. The cost to me was very nearly my life.

"From each according to her ability, to each according to her needs" was proving pretty pricey. In practical terms, the Marxist meter counted on me contributing nursing knowledge, skills and youthful energy but didn't register any needs on my part. Receiving no remuneration for full-time work other than rations insufficient at keeping body and soul together, I was failing my grandmother and mother in their ever-deepening poverty. *Búp's* parting cash gift was long since depleted. *Chợ Rẫy's* celebrated collegiality had been sapped

by political correctness. Since I had fallen under suspicion –
American connection and all, I found no grounds for trusting
others either. "Liberation" had unsettled us; like thousands
of Vietnamese, adrift today in the absence of possibilities
tomorrow, I began to think of taking to the sea. Since childhood
I had struggled against suppression by squashers of hope and
stompers on promise. As a young woman, I saw oppression
across my entire homeland, not just in my mother's home, and
I wanted none of it.

From his sick bed, a smooth-talking operator almost won
me over to walking to Thailand. While I switched his IV bags,
the prospective guide with a gastrointestinal infection plied
me with assurances of his expertise at skirting Vietnamese
authorities, crossing the Cambodian border, avoiding
antagonistic Khmer Rouge, outwitting extortionists, bandits
and the like. Khmer Krom in the Mekong delta quite believably
had networks in the country to our west. He professed to be
indebted to me for my nursing care. Despite a discount, I
would still owe his fee for service. I wavered. We had no mutual
acquaintances, this conductor of fugitives and I. I hesitated.
His infection worsened; the plot dissolved. Incongruous peace
settled upon my indecisive soul. It was not my time.

A loose network of disgruntled nurses and one doctor
gathered occasionally at dusk on park benches or around a
mobile noodle stand. *Lan* was a discontented colleague on the
surgery unit. Newly wed, she drew me aside one evening. A
visitor of one of *Lan's* patients had offered my fellow nurse one
seat on a soon-to-be-outbound boat. The escape was intended
as soon as the patient was discharged, perhaps in three days,
seven at most. Lan was unwilling to be separated from her

husband and the organizers refused to squeeze him in as an additional adult. If I accepted responsibility to care for the recuperating woman and to provide a stock of syringes, sterile scissors, IV solution and more, no gold would be required for my passage. *Lan* helped herself to sterilized and sealed equipment; our physician friend gathered bags of saline and glucose solution. Two days later I took a bus ride to *Cần Thơ* with a young girl and a woman slightly older than I was. We "sisters" received a signal at the bus depot and tailed a fellow to a safe house where we waited an interminable forty-eight hours. After the third nightfall, a bird call drew us to the former patient and her family with whom we lay half-hidden under a canopy as a sculler rowed his boat down the *Hậu Giang* River. Three more runaways boarded and rolled under the tarp. I lay back staring up at the stars in the moonless sky. The heavenly beauty dazzled me. Was I finally free to do as I wished? I stretched out my hand and ran my fingers through the gently lapping water. All was calm. All was right. This waterway was going to sluice me clear of the soil of my people. I breathed deeply. My lungs could not get enough of this air, humid and cool, the nocturnal breath of Vietnam.

What were we waiting for? The boatman had ceased rowing. That flashing light, was it an indication to come or a warning sign? Several hours passed. The man at the tiller admitted he had lost his bearings. How could he have messed this up? I considered how important my presence might be to the rest of the entourage. I reconsidered whether I wanted my life in the hands of this aimless oarsman. He was growing increasingly edgy.

"Let me off."

At dawn he did. I abandoned all the medical supplies and leapt ashore. With relief, I made my way back to *Cần Thơ* just in time to catch a *Hồ Chí Minh* City-bound bus that got me back to the hospital for my next shift. My accomplices at the hospital had expected to witness turbulent reactions to my unscheduled absence. Instead I caught the on-call physician off guard with a telephone message.

"I have a patient here in the ER, Doctor, and I need an opinion from you as soon as possible."

"Is that you, Hanhtiet?"

"Who else? And this patient needs your attention."

When Doctor *Mai* turned up, she stared at me. I smiled inscrutably, held open a patient's file and pointed to the note I had inserted.

"Six o-clock at our customary corner."

My collaborators would have to wait to be debriefed.

Twenty minutes with a gunshot victim drew me into another elaborate escape scheme. The ashen-faced patient had been shot in the side of his chest. As I prepped him for surgery, I talked him through each step in the procedure, disclosing the possibility that his lung had been punctured and was filling with blood. Odd the details one remembers. As I cut off his clothes, I noted the man wasn't wearing the usual loose cotton shorts under his trousers. Close-fitting, legless briefs exposed some out-of-country connection. Ten days later, the man reappeared in the ER. He had made his way from the fourth floor thoracic surgery unit asking for me by name. After offering profuse appreciation for saving his life, *Châu* introduced himself as a former employee of Shell

Oil. He remembered reading my name tag while I had been tending to him.

"I've been looking for you for a few days. Could I come back and see you afterwards?"

I interpreted this request as a flirtatious quip and tried to put him off. *Châu*, however, was insistent and I eventually agreed he could drop by.

A few months passed before a healthier Châu returned to Emergency to arrange a rendezvous in a street-side café. My part in his recovery was apparently motive enough for him to reveal and include me in plans for a breakaway by boat. His wife and children along with families of the other plotters were awaiting calmer seas in the coming weeks. I pled lack of gold. The going price was 3 ingots. Châu said he would explore negotiability with the other organizers. Did I have even one tael? I was cautious. People easily cheated each other for less than thirty-some grams of gold.

Nevertheless, the possibility of release from the prison my country had become stirred hope.

Within weeks *Châu* showed up again. I was welcome to join despite my nearly empty pockets. The ace in my hand was my medical skill. Would I play it? Indifferent was how I wished to be seen. For all I knew, the whole scheme was a ruse. I had my own stories to spin. Once my request for a week off work in *Biên Hòa* Province was approved, I committed to the plan.

My destination wasn't entirely a fabrication. The confluence of the *Đồng Nai* and Saigon rivers was just south of my native island so some waters swirling by the city wharves had already flowed past my grandmother's home. *Châu's* first little scow wasn't heading upstream though. Enroute to a larger seaworthy vessel, we were sighted and chased down river, thumping at maximum speed, outrunning the police before the Saigon flowed into the East Sea. By then the over-taxed engine was kaput. After three days bobbing in Vietnamese waters, carried southwest on the currents, seasickness had emptied every stomach. The condition of the ringleader's two tiniest children, dehydrated and dry-heaving, convinced that former military man to turn back. He knew that if he were detected on re-entry, he faced the prospect of a second stint in Marxist re-education.

We women and the children crammed into the shallow hold. On deck the quasi-cargo of melons and coconuts rolled with the waves. Another boat was spotted. The three men sang folk tunes as one strummed a battered guitar. Casually they asked the fishers for a tow. The skipper on the trawler was no fool and angled for a better payoff. Into the delta we were tugged and let go. A boat with so many people piling off it was a magnet for the coast guard. I splashed to shore and ran the opposite way from everyone else. Returning to the river, I nestled among reeds in the shallows. I heard shouts of the authorities, whimpering kids, and baying dogs. How many of my fellow travelers were rounded up I could not see in the darkness but, as silence fell, I sensed I was safe from arrest. The wind and tide rose. I clung to the brush, shivering, famished and afraid.

At dawn, I spied a few people ambling along the path above the river bank. My damp, rumpled clothing was no great disguise and my urban accent gave me away as soon as I opened my mouth but a morning market vendor pointed the way to a bus on the *Rạch Giá* line. I tramped along beside her wondering at the magnificence of the sunrise. The sky aglow was breathtaking.

"What are you looking for?" I asked myself. "Just what do you think you're doing?"

Trying to flee my misery, my *Má*, my people, and my country had resulted only in days and nights of terror. Had I done wrong? Right? This excruciating self-questioning continued as I silently trailed the locals but vanished as I merged with the crowd at the market. No sellers refused my coins. I wolfed down a mandarin, guava, breastmilk fruit and a bowl of noodles.

Inter-city public transport was in high demand and short supply. The queue for seats was lengthened by shrewd capitalists who lined up early to scalp tickets to travelers like me who had to get on that bus at any price. A young ticket-holder caught my eye and I caught his. I put on my cool bartering persona.

"Is it real?"

I teased him about the authenticity of the ticket in his hand.

"Why should I believe you?"

"You're talking to an honourable gentleman," he countered, "trained at the National Health Institute no less. A more trustworthy citizen you will not find."

"If true," I smiled condescendingly knowing there had been no male students, "you must recognize me as one of your instructors."

The crowd around us, all ears, began to titter.

"Too bad, I called your bluff."

I went in for the kill and acquired the ticket at only double, not triple, its face value. Without bickering, the flush-faced seller took my offer and vanished.

My weary head rested against the bus window. Relatively unscathed, I began my return journey to *Hồ Chí Minh* City. Destiny, I sensed, was at work. I had a vague feeling of being shielded and shown the way. No one had coached me in what to do. Someone beyond sight had steered me out of trouble's oncoming trajectory. I wasn't wily enough to have survived this escapade without a scratch nor smug enough to have assumed so.

People, I reflected, would try to turn anything to their own advantage. That youth hadn't known whom he was dealing with. I had detected weakness in him. He knew I knew he lied. He didn't know what more I had on him. Suddenly I saw myself in a new light. From a gullible country girl, the last four years had toughened me into an astute reader of character, canny and strong. Like unforeseen events in a page-turner paperback novel, my rapid maturation caught me by surprise. A transformation so unimaginable was as inconceivable to me as a happy ending.

Unfathomable

In the city, inflated prices and the fixed stipend of *Chợ Rẫy* nurses eventually meant I simply could not live on my meagre pay. *Hồ Chí Minh* had bequeathed his name and his brand of Marxism to millions. One legacy of decades of warmongering was our remaking as a nation of dealers and brokers. When packages from my sister eventually made it through customs and, via the *Ấn* family, to me, I had stock to trade. Tubes of toothpaste, bottles of aspirin divvied up by the tablet, or lengths of fabric were items I took into, not out of, market stalls. Astute Mrs. *Ấn*, for years a charge nurse at *Chợ Rẫy*, knew when to exchange *đồng* for gold. I never collected enough paper money to afford an ingot. Instead, I saved for twenty-four carat jewelry. Ten such rings were about the equivalent of an ounce of the precious metal.

There was no more danger in the underground economy than in the official one, and definitely greater reward for effort. Whenever I had cash, I set up a pop-up shop myself. My perch was a sturdy cardboard carton with 'Alka Selzer' boldly emblazoned on the side. This empty case I had kept after unpacking supplies at the hospital. People whose portable wealth in pharmaceuticals lacked liquidity bartered away their medications for *đồng*. My street-purchased legitimate drugs went into my box until I could take a trip upcountry. I knew a nurse fifty kilometres away who survived by charging for otherwise unavailable medical care and selling black market medicines. This irregular trade supplemented my paltry income well enough to hazard arbitrary police searches on the buses. Officers pawed through ten kilogram buckets of beans or sacks of sugar belonging to my fellow passengers. From time to time they confiscated some or all of the resold meds in my bag. If anyone talked back, an enforcer would strike. There was no point in protesting. The loser had already lost.

I kept looking for a conduit out of Vietnam. Sporadic, superficial communication from *Búp* assured me that she and the children were well. Letters from me included lists of items to send. The censors in the Post Office must have scanned hundreds of such orders every day; overseas remittances in kind from capitalist emigres were fueling Vietnam's communist economy. Occasionally I added enigmatic confidences to the usual bland expressions about *Má's* health or mine.

"After we finish the memorial for ancestors, *Má* says I can go to visit Uncle *Thái*."

We had no Uncle *Thái*. An acquaintance of mine trusted my sister to settle the passage debt for three thousand US dollars if we landed successfully in a safe haven so he included me in his scheme to evade coastal watchdogs.

The dozen strangers who huddled in a *Vũng Tàu* marsh after nine at night had no excuses when the police searchlights blinded us. What plausible reason besides attempting an illegal departure did we have to be lurking so close to shore? All chance to evade capture evaporated. A handful of officers prodded us toward the local police station scoffing at our folly.

"Idiots!"

Their cold faces taunted. "Your destination is the clink."

Trudging along, I advocated for myself to myself.

"I have done nothing criminal. It's not as if I am a murderer."

By some twist of fate, I had fallen into the hands of these mockers.

"Some con man's laughing all the way to the bank with your gold. You've been fleeced!"

We were about to be shaken down. At the lock up, form filling, the hallmark of systems that substitute checkmarks for actuality, presumed fault. Remorse had more to do with indignity than guilt. Whether confession preceded or arose during interrogation was immaterial. The females in our sorry troupe landed in a one cell, crowded, filthy and sticky. One hundred percent humidity and thirty-six degree heat within brick walls and under a metal roof bred skin irritations and other ailments.

"If they feed me, I'll get through today."

I talked myself through three months incarceration until the *Vũng Tàu* constabulary concluded that this orphan, as I had resolutely self-identified, would never be bailed out by deep-pocketed relatives. In the end, they threw me out.

When I reappeared in the city, there was no place for a traitor such as I was deemed to be at the state institution where I had worked and lived for five years. It was almost midnight when I rattled the barred door below the *Âns'* bedroom. This childless couple, both professionals but without places to serve our topsy-turvy society, had been ferreting out escape routes for their many nieces and nephews. They expected other news from afar about me, not from me face-to-face. I couldn't get in off the narrow laneway without hollering up to them. The walls had ears.

"Brother. Sister. It's me!"

"So, has your mother finally recovered?" Mr. Ấn bellowed fiction for nosy neighbours to repeat as he creaked down the stairs and raised the iron grill that sealed out the night.

"I was worried. You were so late in returning!"

Inside, their faces showed anxiety at not knowing what had become of me.

"I didn't ever want to see your face here again," Mrs. Ấn whispered with characteristic irony, enfolding me into a tight embrace.

"You must be hungry," she spoke louder pulling me into the kitchen and clanging pots and pans to cover further conversation.

Although the Ấns remained a refuge for me, I couldn't accept being a permanent burden on anyone. I began an indigent existence, sleeping on friends' floors and changing houses often. Having no fixed address also described my next occupation, book peddling. Underemployment meant that plenty of people had plenty of time to read. My niche market was literature in French or English. Haggling with both buyers and sellers of foreign language material started many an interesting conversation. Sometimes too interesting. One morning a man in civvies parked his bike next to my sidewalk wares, flipped through some titles and rode off. Soon he returned telling me my business was illegitimate and announcing that he was confiscating all my books. He ordered me to pack up the lot and to follow him to his bureau. I sat out the rest of the day, submitted the requisite self-criticism, and was released empty-handed. I turned again to purchasing pills, capsules, tablets, syrups and serums. The orders from my rural associate were a challenge to fill. Every five to ten minutes beat cops might swagger down the street. I had to be on my toes, relocating my roost ahead of them. Out in the rural provinces, my friend would compensate me for covering house calls with her for a few days. Everything from midwifery to palliative care was available for a price. Pay in kind fed healing hands. Money was hard to come by. Sometimes I stretched the equivalent of five dollars over two weeks. Being an outsider to the Party, I had no political or familial collateral on which to earn a living. I was barely getting by.

By 1982, the world was well acquainted with boat people. Vietnam's Chinese had dug deep to purchase passage out of the country that washed its hands of them, turning a blind eye to outbound vessels when palms were greased with gold. Floating booty made piracy a growth industry in the South China Sea. Under no circumstances did the Áns want me to contemplate escaping toward Thailand, Malaysia or Indonesia. Counterintuitively it seemed, Mr. Ấn investigated routes north through longer-held communist regions.

It was a blistering August afternoon when Mrs. Ấn insisted on accompanying me to the Bình Triệu train station with her husband. Acute melancholy came over me. In the past I had been eager to set out once I had pledged my part in some escape plan. That day was different. I clung to my friends.

"I don't want to leave."

"Crazy girl. Go!"

The couple pushed me from the platform up the stairs into a car. Through tears I watched them wave as whistles blew, pistons hissed, cranks and coupling rods clinked and clanged. All 960 kilometres to *Đà Nẵng*, my feverish head throbbed. I interpreted my physical and emotional condition as signs that this attempt was ill-chosen. For three days in a safe house between the steep Annamite mountains and the coastal plain, I thought only of going home. When I voiced my misgivings to my host, she responded just as Mrs. *Ấn* had.

"Crazy girl!"

Wet season was coming to an end. The squalls and typhoons of the rainy months were weakening, reducing the risks of setting out for the British territory of Hong Kong. The woman walked me to the market where she pointed out a fellow traveler.

"Follow that woman in that hat."

She, whose face and head were concealed by a conical *nón lá*, in turn followed a couple more characters. For all I knew, I had been identified to others now trailing me. All alone, and yet together, our band of about-to-be-fugitives zigzagged our way through the port town. I traveled light upon the road from city to seaside.

A three-wheeled minibus approached. Someone flagged it down. I boarded the *xe lam* behind the iconically-hatted woman, paying my fare wordlessly with only a nod to the driver. No sense speaking in a southern accent here on the central coast. There were already a couple passengers on the two inward facing benches bolted to the chassis over the rear tires. The driver had a full load by the time we were lurching into twilight. The passengers included three more men and four children. I recognized the three boys and one girl, aged eight to twelve, as nephews and niece of Mr. *Ấn*. One was the son of a former officer in the South Vietnamese armed forces. Little *Văn's* father had taken his own pistol to his head rather than be captured by the *Việt Cộng. Tô, Tỷ* and Tina's father had been in re-education for years. They were, therefore, of suspect background and ineligible for anything past primary schooling. Their Uncle *Sáu*, a young man whose laid-back manner concealed his own ex-political prisoner status, chewed on a toothpick and closed his eyes to the dust whirling up in our wake. At the end of the *xe lam* line, we all continued moving, not quite as one. There were thinner crowds along the city's outskirts than at its core where I had felt inconspicuously anonymous.

From behind, a bicyclist rang his bell and passing us, yelled in jest, "Where are you all going? Trying to escape?"

I couldn't imitate the central Vietnamese tones and held my peace. Since he got no response, the nosy bike rider repeated his query.

Someone said he was walking home from the cinema. Had the man on the bicycle seen the latest film?

When he eventually pedaled out of sight, the leaders motioned everyone off the road and into knee high grass.

The pace picked up. I began to panic that I would lose sight of the guide. I jogged closer but not too close. I walked. Ran. Ambled. Sprinted. Stumbled. Picked my way across rolls of barbed wire. Bit my tongue when spikes poked my legs or pierced my fingers. Disentangling myself, I heard children cry out. Had we been jeopardized? Had locals or coastal security recognized something was afoot?

I kept my eyes on the silhouette of the black-clothed trail-blazer. Experience told me not to stick too closely to the pack. When a head-count was taken, I crouched to catch my breath. Thirty-eight of us. Although there was no moon, I could make out higher dunes now above the isolated beach on which we hunkered down. Murmurs passed the word.

"Stay in the shadows. Wait for a signal from the water."

My eyes bored into the darkness surf-side. Breakers were rolling, white water spraying momentary droplets of light into the night. I realized rain and not salty mist was falling on my face. The breeze ruffled my self-restraint. I breathed anxiety. My wristwatch ticked off painfully protracted minutes. Eight thirty. Was the boat late? Eight thirty-three. Where is it? Eight forty-five. There, a flash of light. We crept toward water's edge. The four Ấn children waded in in front of me. Tiny Tỷ couldn't swim. I seized him by the hair and mouthed to the others to grip each other by the hand and hang on to me.

The boat was smaller than promised, just a twenty-five footer fishing craft. Already the men were turning it. I boosted Tỷ into the bow and lifted in the other three. I was hugging the side as the boat began moving. Some of our group were still in the water. I swung my leg over the gunwale just as shots were fired from shore. My fear of being left floundering in the waves was worse than my fright of being hit. I slid in beside the engine which sat a third of the way from the stern.

Around me shouts.

"Stop!"

"Don't shoot!"

"If you do, we'll all die!"

Toward us, from five or six shadowy figures on the dunes, volleys of bullets.

Beside me, a man crawled closer to the engine.

"We've gotta get beyond rifle range."

Male voices cursed steel and starter until ignition. I wriggled out of the operators' way toward the rudder. Rounds peppered the hull.

Pop!   Pop!   Pop!   Pop!   Pop!   Pain. The bullet that entered my belly kept on flying. I sensed it exit smidgens before my right hip. With a smack that echoes still, two others seared abrasions across skin, mementos more indelible than tattoos, burning hotter, longer than the blood pooling beneath my back. Was this the temperature of death? An irregular pulse pounded in my ears almost drowning out the throbbing engine that propelled us further into a darkness darker than dark. I passed out, not away. We were going, getting away. Finally. It was the fifteenth of August, 1982. I was floating in and out of consciousness off the coast of Đà Nẵng. My fingers found the perforations before my lips found my voice.

Faint, my sea-salted tongue called, "Somebody...help me...I am hurt."

The man at the helm heard.

"There's a woman hurt down here. Does she have any family aboard?"

Sáu inched his way over.

"Hanhtict? Where are you wounded?"

Having lost his bag of personal belongings in the rampage out to sea, *Sáu* slipped off his t-shirt, tore it in strips and secured my own bullet pocked towel under the cotton bands.

From time to time, he wrung my blood from the improvised dressing. As for me, it was best to stay still. My right leg felt numb, immobile.

"I don't know if I'll make it," my heavy tongue told *Sáu*. "Sealed in plastic in my bag is a paper. With my sister's address. Let her know. Please."

Sáu comforted me with words of hope. The *Ấn* children, all the children, were okay. Sixteen little ones, from an infant to fourteen years of age were unscathed. I later learned nine of the twenty-two adults had taken lead. Next to me lay a profusely bleeding man. Had no one noticed him? I asked *Sáu* to request towels to bandage his wounds. An open fracture split his shin. I knew he desperately needed surgery. Within wan cheeks, he gritted his teeth. All through the night the maw of death yawned above the deck awash in blood and salt. Was this stranger the one I'd trail into the world of the dead?

Does death come so artlessly upon all people? Is this passing away, this ebbing?

Knowing I was dying, I waited. Had my recent reluctance to make yet one more attempt at escape been a premonition that I would be leaving not only my land but this life?

How effortless is death. Like birth, it is a matter of a will not my own.

I reckoned that this last rite of every life had not been inevitable, not fated for me at that precise moment, but was a logical consequence of distance from the sacraments of surgery. My mind's eye saw my body drifting through the ocean. Cast out upon the swells, sinking, sharks would scavenge visible me. I would become invisible far, far below, far from everywhere that anyone had ever seen.

I slept. I woke.

"Where am I? Have I died? Or do I live?"

The sound of a motor, a sight of the sun, these signs settled me. I remained in the man-made world of manufactured death turning under an immortal sky. How could it be? I wondered next not at dying but at living.

And this is an unfathomable wonder, that flesh and bone and blood and breath come together, alive with sense and spirit.

In brightening dawn I strained to sit up. *Sáu* braced my back and peeled back the cloths. I made a self-assessment. Skin and flesh were torn but no bones shattered. My intestine, if not intact, was not protruding. Movement wasn't helping though. Seepage rinsed, the wet, now salty, fabric was reapplied against my wounds.

Next to me, I saw life leave my nameless neighbour. His eyes had never re-opened. I closed mine. His death was confirmed in a discussion somewhere over our heads. No one wanted to discard the deceased in the sea. It was decided to bury him on Hainan Island which we should pass on our northward voyage through the Gulf of Tonkin. And so I lay those days next to a stiff and swelling corpse.

Throughout that first day at sea, the pilot called out to me from time to time, whether out of mercy or to measure what life was left in me I do not know. No food or communal kegs of water had been loaded in the melee of our disorderly departure but parents of small children took pity on me.

"As a last favour to a dying woman," they said.

A cup was brought to my lips. My nurse eyes estimated forty or fifty millilitres. They accounted, in part, for me making it through a second night.

At daybreak on the seventeenth of August, my speculating tipped from demise to endurance. Also surviving was a twenty-two year old whose skull had been grazed just above his ear. Another had taken a bullet through his palm. Still another had been hit in the upper arm. We lay listless, unprotected from the burning sun. Dust and dirt dismayed me. Above all else, each gash and laceration required cleanliness. At night, the rain, fresh and cool, soothed us until shivers set in. The able men took turns bailing, bailing, bailing, night and day. Meanwhile my bladder refused to empty.

Three or four days out, I heard we were approaching an island. While several people attended to the burial of the deceased, I asked *Sáu* to carry me into the surf. Freed from the rocking of the boat and the rumble of the engine, I rinsed caked blood and grime from my clothes and hair. Once immersed, urine trickled into the sea and I felt a burden lift, yet I could not support myself. Although I could wiggle my toes, my right leg was not cooperating. There was no sensation in the thigh. Wretched leg. Not knowing why I couldn't lift it bred apprehension about permanent injury and disablement. Those fears were swamped as winds and waves rose. Were we going to perish in a storm?

Fearing for my life was then a constantly recalibrated dread. Death I had met. Each new fright, it occurred to me, was felt only by the living. As the dead show no alarm, in an odd sort of way, terror was a vital sign.

Vibrating in its casing to my right, the pulse of the boat's engine never tired while all around me worn and weary travelers wished themselves anywhere but at sea. The skipper had estimated one more day's sailing to British territory when someone sighted a larger but slower vessel ahead of us. Before we came alongside, shouted inquiries were returned with answers that in their hold as well as under the deck canopy was a sizeable cargo of other refuge-seeking Vietnamese. Like us, they had set out from *Đà Nẵng*. Unlike us, they had food and water. They agreed to take all thirty-seven of us aboard. In rough seas, the transfer took time and ingenuity.

"Lower your net."

Two of my fellow travelers pitched me into the knobbly fishing mesh. Those above hoisted me up and fished me out of the ropes. They offered water all around and sliced, dried sweet potato enough. Kindness began its restorative work.

Within hours, we entered Hong Kong territorial waters. The coast guard, into its eighth year of intercepting asylum seekers from a united Vietnam, approached. English words were exchanged. Someone spied the bloodied, bandaged ones among us and radioed for an ambulance boat which didn't dally. Closing in on the port, hands reached out to steady unsteady me. To heal and to hold, paramedics and guards whisked eight injured persons away from our companion strangers. So there I was, in the middle. But also at both an end and a beginning.

Tell My Sister Where I Am

Every medical professional who examined me or my case was baffled. How was I, this forty-five kilogram parched bundle of neurons, tendons, muscles and bone not dead? My abdomen was a massive amber bruise around the shallow shaft bored by the bullet shot right through me. It had sheared two centimetres short of my uterus, the closest major organ. The burn of the second slug was etched permanently across the bruise. An x-ray revealed a third bullet lodged beneath. I was fully conscious of the improbability of my condition as I signed consent for surgery to remove it in Kowloon's Queen Elizabeth Hospital.

Sanitized and sutured, I regained consciousness in the Custodial Ward. In Vietnam, I had served seven years in a fine hospital. In lieu of an insufferable fine for attempting to leave my homeland, I had served three months in jail. Here I was the guest of Hong Kong Correctional Services, iron bars at every window and locks on every door.

Not that I was going anywhere; I hadn't found my land legs. My bed seemed to rock as if pummelled by rolling breakers. I clung to the bedrails, queasy and retching. Hanging on a bed post was a sealed bag with the remnants of my blood-clotted clothing, my only earthly goods. After seven days with almost no food and little water, I was dehydrated and unable to relieve myself. Leaning on the crutch parked by my cot, several times a day I lurched to the open toilet. The strain of squatting and rising under constant surveillance did nothing to ease constipation.

My symptoms of seasickness persisted. During one bout, I heard a Chinese-accented Vietnamese bass voice on the women's ward. Rather than open my eyes and be hammered by woozy vertigo, I did not respond. Only a quarter of the twenty beds were occupied, three by Cantonese speakers with whom I could not communicate. The fourth was a young girl who had been sent to QEH from one of Hong Kong's refugee camps; she was recovering several beds over from mine. The teen told me later her visitor had been a Catholic priest who attended to spiritual needs in that camp. He returned two days later.

This time I was alert and purposeful. "Could you tell my sister where I am, please?"

Sensitive to restrictions and permissions required within the penal system, the priest asked for and got the official go-ahead. He then brought paper and pen, and posted my letter, tucking inside the envelope his own note explaining to Mrs. Lemon where Miss Le was.

Once she received it, *Búp* telegrammed Mr. *Ấn* who had been anxiously monitoring nightly BBC broadcasts. On August 22, he had heard of the Hong Kong landing of forty or so including some severely injured. However, the passage he had negotiated for his siblings' children and for me had been for a band of about two dozen. Had greedy organizers added passengers in a bid to boost their profits? Deviations from the original plan may have let secrecy slip and exposed us to those gunslingers along the coast.

On the priest's next round, he inquired if there was anything I needed. I began cautiously with the obvious.

"I'm lying here with nothing to do. There's not a thing to read."

He pulled out a single volume in Vietnamese, everything else in his brief case was in Chinese characters. Roman Catholic creeds and prayers were definitely a departure from my former literary diet of mystery, ghost and adventure novels. Heavenly-minded catechism proved to be a short-lived distraction from excessive self-examination as to how I had landed in this bind.

A more prickly predicament than nonexistent reading material was the lack of undergarments. Granted, I was more familiar with Buddhists, Caodaists or Taoists, but presumably a celibate holy man of any persuasion shouldn't be asked to think about, let alone touch women's underwear. For a time I couldn't bring myself to broach the subject; to mention unmentionables to him mortified me. Eventually, blushing, I asked him if I might ask him to help me with personal items.

"Whatever you need."

"Is it too much to ask for underclothing?"

Visions of robed bonzes or collared clerics sizing up lingerie in an open-air market were nothing if not absurd.

"However could he find some?" I wondered.

Caritas had sisters as well as brothers in Hong Kong. A charitable nun shopped on my behalf. Within days I was handed a shopping bag with a pair of thick-soled plastic flip flops, three pairs of panties, a pair of slacks and a button up blouse. The contents of that bag were the sum total of my wardrobe when, after almost four weeks cooped up in recovery, I rejoined my fellow escapees.

One Two Four Three Six Five Four

Chi Ma Wan Detention Camp was barely two months old. Prior to July 1982, asylum seekers who had landed in Hong Kong were housed in "open" facilities from which many commuted to employment in Cantonese or British businesses in Kowloon or the New Territories while waiting for resettlement. In an effort to stem the tide of displaced persons to one of the regions' few remaining safe havens, subsequent arrivals were placed in "closed" camps.

The hour-long ferry ride to Lantau Island restarted my fading seasickness. I relapsed into nauseous immobility while every point of reference bobbed before my eyes. Reopening them only once we reached the public pier, I saw heat shimmering off corrugated metal-clad roofs of long sheds behind twenty-five foot high fences. In the custody of a uniformed escort, several Vietnamese besides me disembarked after a few local passengers. The spiny ridge of the Chi Ma Wan peninsula rose up green behind the buildings. The bay on Lantau's southeastern flank faced the bustling metropolis twenty kilometres away, but at sea level that view was blocked by Hei Ling Chau Island. Inside the enclosure, fifteen hundred refugees watched. Our arrival gave the inmates clustered along the wire barrier something to look at.

Hong Kong Correctional Services registered me and snapped an identification card on my shirt through a buttonhole. How anyone might have wished to self-identify was irrelevant to the system. My initial ID number corresponded to a number assigned to the boat on which I'd made landfall. Three digits added later: 6, 5, 4, were unique to me. Since Vietnamese were commonly nicknamed numerically according to their birth order, there were many people known as *Sáu, Năm,* and *Bốn.* To that combination I would learn to respond as surely as to my given name. Being in Cantonese territory, I also became alert to *"Luhk, Ngh, Sei"* which more often meant me when a camp authority was calling.

The flat terrain of the detention camp included a clinic and industrial modular trailers housing the office of the United Nations High Commissioner for Refugees, temporary embassy delegations, and NGOs – Non Governmental Organizations – the not-for-profit or charitable agencies that were contracted to provide specific services to displaced persons. Numbered huts held extensive banks of three tiered bunks. Worn sheets, threadbare towels or strips of fabric from extra, extra large donated Western clothing hung as curtains cordoning off individual or family spaces from otherwise unobstructed scrutiny. The board on a metal frame beneath and the one above limited each person's space to just over two square metres. Singles and unaccompanied minors got top tier accommodation, in the heat right up under the rafters. I was assigned a spot next to Kim, a young woman who had made it out of *Đà Nẵng* with her little sister.

The rest of my companions at sea soon came by, all smiles that I was on the mend. Our helmsman reminded me then, as he often would, how he had kept hounding me day and night. My conscious responses to his constant "How are you?" had assured him that I hadn't passed out or passed on. How I had made it dumbfounded him. Everyone grew grim at the memory of the man we had lost but all recounted the satisfaction of providing an honourable burial. Barely a month after our ordeal, all the other visible hurt had healed. Invisible injury, whether recent or generations in the making, exhibited itself day in and day out. Family groups never left their bunks unguarded. The camp-issued blankets, scratchy woolen taupe, useful until November as a make-shift mattress and afterwards as a cover against falling temperatures, were ubiquitous and un-alluring. There was no traffic either, in the plastic bowls, mugs and spoons which every internee carried to the mess hall. Acquisitive fingers, however, found every unprotected private possession. Even before I passed through the gates, covetous eyes fixed on the super spongy soles of my new, blue, priest-provided flip flops. The sun-baked, bare concrete was hard on the feet. If I hadn't wrapped my flimsy footwear with a second shirt and used that as a pillow, those flip flops would have walked while I slept.

Standing in line for meals, which were prepared in a communal kitchen by teams of refugees, consumed at least two hours beginning mid-morning and again late afternoon. Out under the tropical sun, monsoon-season humidity sapped my strength as I queued for food, or sheets of toilet paper, or whatever was being distributed. The first meal of the day was lighter, congee with boiled squash or choy, perhaps slices of fried liver, fatty pork or fish. Waiting for it with well-mannered people could make for good conversation;

there was always pleasure in congenial repartee. On the other hand, rude conduct and rough speech soured many a morning. Statelessness had flattened but not eliminated the social hierarchy. Social graces are not erased in adversity, neither are they nurtured. An attitude of entitlement by busy-body scroungers, hardened by a deprived upbringing, put me off. People who had never, absolutely never, ever received anything for free from their government, disdained clothing handouts and took affront when offered common flip flops. To avoid such nastiness, the sticky afternoon air, and the stench of too many bodies in too small a space, I often let the supper column almost entirely file past the canteen servers before I tagged on at the end. Inside the mess hall, as wide as an airplane hangar, food scoopers favoured or deprived at will. If a server was a friend or wanted to befriend you, you would find more meat in your bowl. Otherwise there would be more gristle and grease than animal protein. Children received extra egg rations, oranges too. Pretty girls got chatted up and choice pieces were served with hopes of special favours later. Kitchen hours were long; the work was heavy. The reward was occupation. Some worked to escape their own thoughts; others supplemented their diet. There was no other pay.

Following my first supper, Mr. *Sáu* found me. His classification as a former officer of the army allied with the Americans gave him confidence that his documents and his relatives already in the USA would speed him on his way to resettlement there. Because of his presence, his niece and nephews, all under age, were spared the hazards faced by unaccompanied minors. Many families, seeking to avoid losing everyone on an ill-fated voyage out of Vietnam, split up and sent children alone at different times on different boats.

Camp life was complicated. Privacy was nowhere to be had. Relations between men and women were often awful. Spouses had no spaces for intimacy. Some single men, without the collective constraints of our traditions and watchful extended families, preyed on young women, especially solitary individuals who had no protector. If a man fancied a girl but she refused his advances, she might be stalked. Incessant attempts at unwanted conversation seemed unstoppable, try as she might to insist that, in those circumstances of uncertainty, coupling was neither decent or desirable. We were locked in the embrace of an unexplained international migration system which was going to take months or years to untangle. Sexual appetites, however, knew no such inertia. Pressure tactics by gangster types included violence and vile practices. There were men who avenged the loss of face they perceived in a rebuff by scooping excrement out of one of the open sewers and splattering it over the young lady who had given them the cold shoulder.

Cleaning the communal latrines was one of the duties Chi Ma Wan residents were detailed to do by hut headmen. They never assigned friends to that task. Others were charged with sweeping or spraying down walls and floors. In those weeks, I was still manoeuvering my way around on a crutch. I couldn't manage two-handed tools and passed hours repeating exercises I recalled from therapists at *Chợ Rẫy* hospital. Lifting my right leg, bending and stretching, I concentrated on expanding its range of motion. To overcome my disability became my focus. The future appeared as a murky tunnel.

My goal was resettlement, but where or when I could not see. In the moment, I endeavored to improve my timing and flexibility climbing up to or down from my third tier bunk. I strove for strength and balance to accomplish formerly simple movements such as changing trousers without needing to sit down. Steadying myself under a public shower spigot, I could wash the clothing I was wearing but struggled to peel off wet pants and shirt when shielded from sight only by a blanket held up by another woman. After I dressed in my other blouse and trousers, I pinned the sopping clothes on a line in the sun. To prevent theft, I found a spot in the shade from where to keep an eye on them. Watching laundry dry near a blabbermouth or windbag irked me, but with an interesting raconteur I whiled away hours happily distracted from our situation.

Once a week, hundreds of us sat at the only tables, in the dining hall, writing aerograms distributed, collected and then mailed all over the world. I wrote the *Ăns*.

"We are all healthy including the four children waiting for arrangements for resettlement."

I revealed very little else because in detention I had no other comforting words to share. The last thing I wanted was to compound anxiety for my dear friends whose mail would be examined by strangers before they themselves opened it.

To *Búp*, I felt free to tell more, describing reassuring details of my recuperation but also explaining the complication of being held in a closed camp – a restriction unknown by earlier refugee claimants in Hong Kong.

Before those letters reached my loved ones, and long before they replied to what I thought was my fixed address, "Boat 1243 #654" was paged over the loudspeakers. Along with forty to fifty women, I reported to the hall toting our belongings as ordered. We milled about wondering what was coming, churning out rumours. Would we soon be on an America-bound airplane? I hadn't yet been seen by any immigration delegation. Eventually a United Nations spokesperson announced our transfer to another site. A decision had been taken in light of compromised safety and security of single females in Chi Ma Wan.

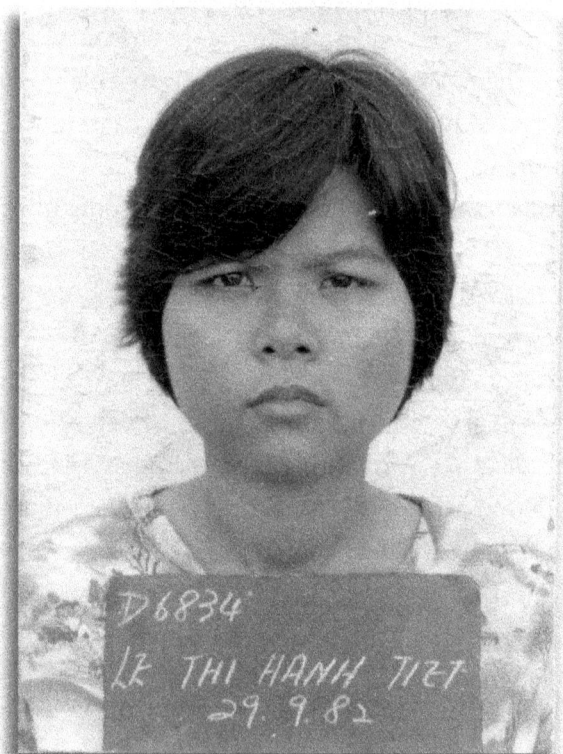

Hanhtiet, 1982, Kowloon, Hong Kong

Kowloon Clink

For the third time in six weeks, I boarded a boat not knowing for certain the destination. Pitching on choppy seas, my stomach hurled its contents. My imagination listed into dangerous territory; I envisioned misfortune raining down on me at any moment. During the hours in transit by ferry and then by bus, the chatter turned to what other camp we might be headed for. No one was prepared for the placard over the door where we were offloaded: Lai Chi Kok Prison for Women in Kowloon.

Prison?

Prison!

Female guards ordered us to form a queue and marched us inside. Paperwork, mugshots, fingerprints, stripsearches. The authorities removed all our belongings including our clothes. In a huge room, a metal detector scanned our naked bodies as we bent over and jumped on command. Nudity was absolutely shameful to us. Utter degradation was what we felt as the women in uniform herded us into a communal shower. For our "protection" we were being treated like animals, divested of human dignity. The water rinsed off dust and sweat but our skin could not repel the disgrace of being among dozens of other unclothed women under the gaze of the guards. From such primitive minds, I expected no good.

We scrambled to cover ourselves when our clothes were returned to us. In street clothes, we were easily distinguishable from convicts who wore institutional garb. Our shoes were confiscated; footwear offered too many prospects for running drugs, blades or other contraband into the prison. As we stood stiffly in two parallel lines, another headcount was completed. Then plastic sandals were distributed, avocado in colour and sheared of the heel strap. That was intentional. These slippers flapped against floor and sole, slapping so loudly we couldn't sneak up on anyone. Although we kicked them off at our cell door, the condition of corridor, shower and courtyard floors discouraged us from going barefoot elsewhere. Shoe-share immediately became our habit; from the heap no one could pick out a matched pair let alone a particular set.

The warden addressed us as we stood at attention. Translated by a couple of Vietnamese women among us who spoke excellent English, she outlined prison rules and regulations. Her manner, though reserved, was not unkind. The correctional officers who escorted us to our cells used limited English to issue intelligible orders. None of us yet knew Cantonese.

We moved out of the main building and into a cell block. Out of the rain, we kicked off those glowing green sandals and lined up again. The guards numbered us off twelve to sixteen per cell. Inside mine, two rows of four bunk beds flanked an aisle that ran the length of the room. On each bunk lay a set of pajama-like uniforms. Once more, we, who had woken that morning as strangers in Chi Ma Wan, were indecorously required to simultaneously undress and put on these inmate uniforms. The cotton tops had capped shoulders, no sleeve to speak of. Mid-thigh-length short pants had no elastic or tie at the waist. We learned, with more or less success, how to twist the waistband and tuck it in to keep the shorts up. We surrendered any belongings still on our persons.

That night I lay uncomfortably on the plank beneath my back. The single coverlet didn't provide much padding or warmth. Everlasting questions, especially "Why?" - the quintessence of humanness, marched incessantly through my sleepless mind. By the clock, guards unlocked the grill that formed the short wall along the corridor. They banged loudly on the bars to make every occupant turn and uncover faces toward the beam of their flashlights while they counted heads.

Sleep came in fits and starts. Between the sentries and deposits in the nightsoil bucket in the back corner, sustained silence was rare. Never in our lives had any of us slept in a privy. Now no walls or windows shielded us from nasty smells and sounds. Strange how sleep-deprivation exaggerated sensitivities. A stream of urine rushing, dribbling or pinging into a metal drum echoed across cinder-block walls. Offensive odors produced by only one cellmate stricken by diarrhea when we'd all eaten the same food started middle-of-the-night conversations and medical consultations. How could the most stunningly beautiful body emit the vilest stench? Twelve wide-awake women tittered, cackled or crowed in the darkness. We laughed the laughter of the rattled. Our mirth was edgy not merry. The day's emotional pendulum had swung from blissful hope to incredulous shame.

After we had quieted ourselves, the creak of the restless turning on a bed board here and there was interrupted by a rhythmic "Pshhhh. Ut. Pshhhh. Ut. Pshhhh. Ut."

Someone whispered toward the unhearing fisherwoman snoring on an upper bunk, "Momma, pleeeease let us sleep."

Come morning, the sleepless were more direct.

"I'm not going to spend another night listening to you wuffle and snuffle while I can't sleep. If you're in the bunk above me, I'll kick your butt from below until you bounce right off."

At the sound of a bell, our entire cell block emptied into the concrete yard. All four dozen of us Vietnamese queued up before being escorted to the canteen. We could see the convicted through a series of chain link fences but you would have had to holler to carry on a conversation with any of them. Yelling wasn't part of our day. Meals were dished out with decorum; servings were sufficient, even generous. Between meals, it was up to us to find some way to pass the time. I walked laps in the courtyard, still limping. Around tables in the dining hall, six to eight women gathered, playing chess, checkers or other games. Chow Yun-fat, Sammo Hung, Bruce Lee and other avengers killed and kicked their way through kung-fu flicks projected on a wall. One of our number, a teacher by training, endeavoured to offer us English language lessons. She had no materials at first, not even paper or pencils.

Daily metal searches turned up a stick pin once. In a neighbouring cell, a young lady had ingeniously crafted a sewing needle. Drawing threads from clothing, she could do repairs or replace loose buttons. We admired her initiative;

I revered her amazing inventiveness. When discovered, the authorities classified her as cunning rather than clever.

Other than that incident, the correctional staff noted that we as a whole made no trouble. After several weeks, we were given an aerogram each. On the flimsy blue foldable paper, I wrote my sister of my relocation and of my good health. I had nothing good to say about my leg. My scabs and abdominal sutures however, had sealed well. I felt the burnished skin around the puckered scars while washing in the abominable group showers that continued day after day.

My optimism was forced. I willed myself to look on the bright side and avoided voicing questions that plagued me. Why were we in prison? How long would we languish there? Three months after being received in a domain of first asylum we had yet to be seen by a representative of the United Nations High Commission for Refugees. Would we spend our lives there with no answers? Our confinement wasn't a secret. Those aerograms which we submitted unsealed were pasted shut and posted on our behalf.

One day in November, my name was included in the list of those with incoming mail. We were called from the canteen to an office. One by one the women ahead of me were ushered behind a closed door to have envelopes or packages opened and presented under watch. When I reached the head of the line, I was turned back and, without explanation, returned to the dining hall.

As I settled back in the crowd, with no answers to queries about what I had received, my bewilderment grew. An English-speaking Vietnamese, who was often called upon to translate, was paged. She returned some time later holding a carry-on travel case crammed full of undies, a couple tops and pairs of pants and candies. She offered all the women at our table a share of the chocolate.

Six or so weeks into our stay at the prison, an announcement was given to our entire group.

"Get ready."

For what? We could see the cleaning crew had done some spectacular work on the canteen; the dining hall certainly was spruced up.

For who?

"A special guest."

The only visitor we wanted was someone with authority from the UNHCR. The woman who was presented to us had proven credentials; she was a long-term, dedicated advocate for refugees in Hong Kong. Our spirits soared. Someone was going to listen to us.

"How are you being treated?"

The tedium of incarceration was our most common complaint.

"We have nothing to do."

"We're wasting our lives here."

"We are not criminals. Why are we prisoners?" "We want to see foreign delegations screening candidates for resettlement in America, Australia, Canada..."

Our caller spoke comforting words and committed herself to doing her best. Still, she could not confidently say if or when our requests would be granted. All the pop and sizzle of excitement in the room fizzled. My hope deflated like an overstretched, saggy balloon.

That woman was true to her word however, and a few weeks later we cheered at the news that all of us were leaving. All our meagre earthly goods, catalogued and stored at our arrival in October were handed back. Forty-some women enfolded each other in tight embraces. One of our wishes was coming true. We formed the familiar double line for a final time, stepped purposefully over the threshold and clambered aboard a chartered bus. Our destination, back under the auspices of the High Commission for Refugees, was none other than Chi Ma Wan, the closed camp from which we had been dispatched three months earlier. As befitted our abject station in life, we received no explanation from the authorities for this turn of events.

One in Ten Million

Thirty metres up the wooded hillside from the lower camp, another perimeter fence enclosed the grounds of an aging correctional facility. Upper Chi Ma Wan afforded a view of the rooftops and guard towers closer to the shore, and from some spots, a panorama of the sea. It was here that I got my first face-to-face encounter with an international migration specialist. I, of course, was nowhere near the first refugee that particular bureaucrat had examined. Worldwide, more than 325,000 Vietnamese were seeking asylum at the time the UN opened my file in January 1983. The tens of thousands of boat people were just a drop in the bucket; global refugee numbers topped 10,600,000 that year. Most of those claimants were not recent additions to that count. Protection and reception of children, women and men displaced mostly by disasters of human making had peaked. Resettlement procedures were protracted and repatriation was fraught with resistance. None of this was made known to me. Instead, I walked smack into a rule-bound stance familiar the world over. Systems, composed as they are of interconnected arrangements, assorted sets, and series of subsets, feast on pattern. Recognition by category or classification may be a sign of algorithmic intelligence but it wasn't the measure of me. The variables didn't add up.

"Describe your occupation."

I reviewed my transition from nurse-in-training to emergency room professional.

"Explain your reasons for leaving Vietnam."

I tried to articulate the impossibility of living under a regime that had labeled me without knowing me.

"Clarify how your family history fits into this."

I provided every detail I could about *Búp*, George, Daniel, Frank, and Josie.

Weekly interviews followed, focused on family.

"So, now, tell us the truth about this 'half-sister' of yours."

"Give us more details on your relationship with Americans in Saigon."

"What kind of information did you have access to through your relatives that may have been valuable to the intelligence operatives?"

After several hours of this, I felt as if my head would explode. Aside from the repetition made necessary by translation, the probing, always slightly slanted, could have been asked just as easily in Vietnamese as in English. In fact, I had heard these very questions before I fled my homeland. I had suffered for my naiveté about the communists since 1975. It appeared that officials of whatever political stripe: leftist, centrist or rightist, all read from the same interview manual.

My interlocutor stated prospects for resettlement in the USA were bleak. He told me I was over eighteen. That was not news to me. Then he informed me that the woman in California I called my sister couldn't claim me as a dependant. I nodded; I certainly didn't want to be a burden on *Búp*. Our conversation concluded without definitive closure. Falling into the deduction trap, I imagined, based on observable processing times of other detainees, that within about six months I would be reunited with *Búp* and her family.

Upper Chi Ma Wan's cohort of North Vietnamese was ideologically and linguistically different from those of us of southern origin. While my ears adapted to their seven tones, I was particularly suspicious of any Vietnamese who spoke Cantonese too. By turning informant, some curried favour from the guards, few of whom had more than rudimentary English. Negotiating camp relationships was complicated even without a language barrier. Since getting the ear of the authorities without an intermediary seemed strategic, I began to beg a Chinese-Vietnamese interpreter to teach me. All I wanted was twenty minutes of Cantonese lessons every evening for two weeks. The fellow was willing but busy. His wife, with time on her hands, grew perturbed when I would come by their bunk ready for a tutorial. Her agitation, I decided, was not my concern, whereas my self-defence was.

"Thicken your skin," I said to myself and ignored her dirty looks.

With keen motivation, I practiced new words daily, attempting conversations with the corrections officers who walked their beat or lounged at their posts out of the heat. Their duties were not onerous and the partners, usually one male and one female, were easily accessible. Perhaps my efforts amused them. I was constantly messing up meaning among monosyllabic words only differentiated by a rising falling tone as opposed to a falling rising one.

Winter in Hong Kong was brutal for anyone from the tropics. In *Đồng Nai*, a temperature of 20°C would have sent me scurrying to put on all the clothes I owned. Twelve degrees latitude farther north, my old January lows were the new highs. I wore second-hand jeans and a donated jacket constantly during days of 14 to 19°C and nights cooler still. A dry, cold wind chafed my ankles; there were no socks to be had, and my chapped hands bled. At the next opportunity to send an aerogram, I asked *Búp's* help. Mindful that a package mentioned in her earlier letters hadn't made it into my hands, I cautioned her.

"Send only a few things. Warm is what I need but slightly worn out rather than brand new might raise the odds of my receiving them."

In her wisdom, my sister sent her second care package exactly as she had the first. Hearing "Boat 1243 # 654" in triplicate: Cantonese, Vietnamese and English, I headed to the hut where officers cut off the knotted string and opened the brown butcher paper wrapping. Inside were several pairs of underwear, two shirts and a couple of pairs of pants. At the bottom of the box I found a bar of chocolate just like the one shared after that odd postal call back at the women's prison. The clothing looked familiar too; I had seen the same shirts and identical trousers on the refugee who had often been tapped to do English translation. When next I noticed her wearing those clothes, I changed into mine and sauntered by.

"Oh my ... we're ... someone sent you the same things..."

Soon afterwards she pulled me into a corner and replayed the Lai Chi Kok parcel delivery scenario as she had experienced it. She offered to give everything, including the shoulder bag, to me. I declined.

"I can't wear four shirts at once. You need tops too."

"How can I repay you?"

In the camps it was better to be owed than to owe. Building social capital was perhaps an even more delicate operation there than in open societies where money could ease the exchange of favours. It dawned on me that the delicate dance equal parties do when cultures intersect graciously was not my lot. Ancient Cantonese custom, with a thin veneer of British rule of law, governed us. Hong Kong prison guards were bound by the intricacies of *guanxi* obligations. Lest they remain obliged to a refugee whose translation skills enabled them to do their work, they had restored the social balance by returning the favour in the form of goods my fellow inmate had lacked. No mind that her gain was my loss. The guards owed me nothing and had absolved their own debt by redirecting the gift *Búp* intended for me. I pondered the meanness which one individual, in order to save face before another, may so indifferently unleash on a powerless third party.

March blew in blustery and wet. Occasional showers, a little rain in the morning, drizzle through the afternoon, thunderstorms in the evening, overcast and humid at night, all added up to no sun. Hundreds of wet garments hung on lines strung up inside. Fabric reeked musty and damp. Clothing never dried. People shivered and sniffled. I bound my gloveless hands in strips of cloth, thankful for *Búp's* thoughtfulness.

Keeping busy kept one's mind off the cold and keeping in motion kept the edge off the chill. A boy scout program was organised to keep idle hands out of mischief. Along with four men, I volunteered to be a scout master. As for credentials, I could draw on my own school-day excursions and medical training. Camp authorities approved of healthy, supervised activity and so we began daily sessions with our boys. I became den mother to ten seven and eight-year olds. Each master prepared and led two hours of camping skills: fire building, sending smoke signals, and the like. First-aid training was my forte. With a congenial guard escort, the scouts were permitted to hike up and down the track just outside the perimeter fence of the camp, climbing trees and even picnicking on the cliffs above the beach. Every active hour was rehabilitative, building up my gimp leg. Meaningful hours strengthened spirits and built bonds, but I held friends loosely. From one day to the next, a little cub's family or even a scout leader's immigration criteria might be met, travel documentation would arrive, and another happy someone could leave the limbo of stateless status behind.

Hanhtiet with refugee students, 1982, Camp Collinson, Hong Kong

The World Should Go On

I saw the last of Lantau Island that May. The powers that be determined that a particular segment of the population would be transferred to Cape Collinson. This time, they gave some advance notice to women without refugee relatives, single young ladies, unaccompanied minors and a few families with children. Only three to four hundred detainees were relocated. Most of these were from Vietnam's northern and central provinces; a smattering of southerners were included. It had been five months since I faced a ferry trip; walking up the gangway triggered all the residual trauma my body associated with sea travel. This time the boat docked at Hong Kong Island itself. Motion sickness hardly abated along the narrow land route of hairpin curves that clung to the coast up to the far northeast.

Getting off the bus with my small satchel, I breathed deeply and easily. Like British Royal Engineer Collinson had done one hundred and forty years earlier, I surveyed a spectacular panorama. The headland facing Tathong Channel opened up vistas of the sea on three sides, a peak at our back, above us only sky, bright and blue and breezy. That openness, grand and constant, spoke to my spirit of good prospects.

Like Chi Ma Wan, Collinson was a closed camp that restricted refugee claimants' movements. However, the local administration wasn't narrow-minded. We could try to improve our lot. To contact American Consular officials in Hong Kong, I wrote letters. I believed I was part of the Orderly Departure Program but did not understand the classification system.

"You have to wait your turn," was all the acknowledgement I was given.

Without knowledge or well-placed contacts, I plunged into activities that occupied my mind as much as my time. Despair was a wily adversary but could be beaten back by busyness. From my arrival, I was on the go almost every day. In the jigsaw of life, puzzle pieces came together. The camp clinic operated by World Relief wanted my medical and language skills. I began translating on site and also accompanying patients to hospital in Kowloon under police escort. Sometimes genial guards took me out for a meal. Lunching at congested noodle counters cheek by jowl with harried workers hurrying back to offices or factories was a complete contrast to the nonstop waiting of statelessness. I was given a ring-side seat on many a medical spectacle; as a peripheral character, my role called more for observation than acting.

Our escort would plan a three to four hour trip around a fifteen or twenty minute specialist appointment. Guards would often squeeze in some personal shopping on the government's time. Since detainees working for NGOs could be paid in kind but not in cash, I was rewarded for my efforts with packets of dried sour plums or shrimp chips. Inside one gynecologist's exam room, I interpreted wisdom, or ignorance, of reproductive health from one party to the other. I marveled at the mysteries of gestation, so beautiful, so elegant, but born within one impulsive young woman heedless of prevention, protection or provision.

These excursions exhausted me. Both the emotional and mental demands were taxing; the rolling ferry trips were punishing. Back inside the camp boundaries, my snacks and sundries became bartering chips. Mothers pressed me with surreptitious requests for salted crackers, thread or toiletries in exchange for the oranges or eggs only kids received from early childhood supplementary feeding programs. My My was the giggling three-year-old daughter of a single mother whose bunk neighboured mine. I was often indebted to her for saving me some supper when outings for medical appointments stretched into the evening. I was beholden to the little tyke for the unconditional affection she showered on me. Words cannot describe how I missed her hugs when the two of them left for the United States.

American poet Carl Sandburg wrote "a baby is God's opinion that the world should go on." Amid the suffering that was, and is, the lot of displaced peoples the world over, the antics of a laughing child can charm cursed or cursing lips into spontaneous smiles. Such is the irrepressibility of hope.

Most days, my responsibilities at World Relief revolved around language teaching and learning. There weren't enough native speakers of English so NGO staff recruited refugees with intermediate or advanced competence. In the morning, my students were adults focused on limited but practical content of English; we constructed sentences aiming for mutual intelligibility. Despite our variable, regional

Vietnamese accents, our mother tongue traits transferred to English; we clipped vowels, omitted syllable-ending sounds, and stumbled over consonant clusters.

Two hour mid-afternoon classes for children covered a wider curriculum. Around twenty kids deemed to be at grade five learned math, Vietnamese literature and folk tunes in addition to English. Some of the young girls who gathered around my tables in the four-hundred seat dining room lived on nearby bunks in the same longhouse. To them and others, I became *Cô Giáo* – Teacher. Although our paths crossed many times a day, my pupils were timid in class. They claimed almost no recall of vocabulary from one day to the next. When translating took me outside and class was cancelled, my pupils rarely joined another of the many simultaneous lessons going on in the hall.

"We can't understand the other teachers."

True, it was hard to hear if you sat on the periphery of fifty to seventy students addressed by one instructor while a few metres away another group was chanting verb conjugations, and behind you a choral reading of poetry vied for your attention. I urged the girls to put effort into reviewing language lessons during their unstructured hours. At ten years of age, how could they see what I realized at twenty-eight? In all my camp duties, there was only gain, never loss. This conviction drove me to perpetually sharpen my skills and deepen my knowledge.

A yearning to understand people, really sensing empathically rather than stopping at simply appraising them, was at work within me. Sometimes I would skip the breakfast line-up and feed on conversation with the guards and officers.

Tending to us was just a paycheque to most of them; paying attention to them enriched my grasp of the world spinning through the 1980s beyond the fence. Their recognition of me had other benefits. For instance, unlike those long and empty hours in Chi Ma Wan, I now had no time to watch out for wash hung to dry. If I appeared too many days in the same shirt and pants, one guard in particular would remark about this and realize that someone had helped themselves to my single change of clothing left unattended on a laundry line. First, she would fume about the scavengers. Then she would direct a lower ranking colleague at the warehouse to give me a change of clothes. Another advantage of being known by authorities for the right reasons was security. Relationships with people of influence sheltered me; no refugees dared to do me harm.

Associates with World Relief who oversaw education programming at Collinson also bonded with refugees like me who volunteered to deliver services in the camp. As the Year of the Pig drew to a close and the Year of the Rat began at the Lunar New Year in February 1984, Kevin advised his dozen or so Vietnamese teachers and sports coaches to skip supper. "Don't line up at the mess hall at 6 o'clock. After everyone else has eaten and left, we'll eat together."

With a twinkle in his eye and a smile, our Aussie boss told us he was going home early but would return. Dusk was falling when we heard a tapping on the camp loudspeaker. The help of World Relief refugee staff was urgently requested. We were to report to the dining hall immediately. Inside, the Dutch and Australian aid workers had put on an incredible spread. The aroma of golden spring rolls, deep-fried to perfection, rice-paper coat just crispy enough and stuffed with savory shrimp, pork strips, grated carrot, onion, cilantro and bean sprouts was heavenly! The food of the gods in a perhaps not God-forsaken place!

I didn't know God. World Relief had been founded as a charitable arm of American churches in 1944 to walk the talk of loving one's neighbour as oneself by bringing humanitarian assistance to victims of the Second World War. In 1984, recruits to short-term relief work in Collinson included a Vietnamese pastor and his wife who had resettled in Australia. They led Vietnamese Christian worship; some North Vietnamese, long isolated from organized religion of any kind, were converted.

During this time, the UNHCR mission made one of its rare rounds and a Canadian immigration delegation came too. Word was that the Canadian quota had been raised. One hundred hard luck cases were accepted in a single day of interviews. *Lai*, one of my English students, flagged me over to where he squatted in the shade near the gate. He was over the moon with the news that Canada had approved his family's application.

"I just converted, Teacher, and now, can you believe it? I'll soon put this refugee hell behind me. You ought to convert too!"

"Convert? To what? To whom? I don't know God."

"It really doesn't matter. Just convert. Show the officials your baptismal certificate. And bingo! You're in!"

A refreshing breeze ruffled my hair and I pinched my blouse away from my perspiration-coated skin.

Several unsettling facts perturbed me about *Lai*'s line of reasoning. I had first come to know him in Chi Ma Wan by his thieving ways. He was a smooth operator lifting clothing from an aid agency warehouse and selling pieces on the sly. Although I had never met God, I couldn't imagine *Lai's* modus operandi aligned with any sacred path. And God, it seemed to me, wasn't one to be impressed, let alone persuaded, by paper credentials.

Bowl and spoon in hand, I joined the line jostling near the canteen. The serving vats had been delivered through the gate from the kitchen facilities up the road. Fish. Again. Fresh from the sea, ample servings, so tasty, yet I ate without gratitude. I did not know then how to lap up the moment. I did not know whom to thank, nor did I think of thanking anyone. Fixated on a future always just beyond my reach, I mostly missed the marvels of present provision. Although the migrant management system barred me from earning wages or accumulating wealth, compassion was feeding and sheltering me. But that wasn't enough.

Twenty families left in one departure. A substantial second group moved on too. Collinson was shrinking. The sky came closer, my horizons lower. In February 1985, the remaining refugees were shunted across the water past Pearl Island, the Gold Coast and Castle Peak, way past.

*S*o Fragile a Promise

In the New Territories, Tuen Mun was grimy and my perspective became grim. Save the Children interviewed the World Relief refugee staff as we were transferred in from Collinson. Teaching children continued to be a strategic distraction from immigration uncertainty although this bigger camp disheartened me and my enthusiasm waned. I was despondent. I felt trapped in an eternal line-up for entrance to America; every transfer seemed to send me back to the beginning of the queue. Letters from *Búp* continued.

"We're working on it. Don't give up."

"No, don't follow-up with that recommendation to apply to Australia. We'll get you here."

Every twenty dollar bill sealed in my sister's envelopes was extracted, accounted for, and placed in safekeeping for me until, well, until I had somewhere else to go. I wandered the grounds a lot. My dormitory was adjacent to the headquarters of an industrial group that offered work to knitters and crocheters. The clicking, clacking cacophony was too much for me so I rarely stayed on my bunk.

Along my circuit around the camp, I crossed paths with a German Buddhist. I had never in my life had a conversation with a monk and I practiced no religion. It was hard to miss this master. The European towered over the Mahayana practitioners of Tuen Mun. His massive, calloused bare feet convinced some of his devotion and venerability. Why then did he touch my elbow? Male female physical contact was *verboten*. I grew curious. What life had he relinquished to join his order? What had he gained? What credence anchored his creed? Master started a conversation with me because he could. In our common second language, he appealed to me to assist in translating teaching to his congregants. But what did I know of Sanskrit? Nothing. Buddhist terminology borrowed from the ancients spoken by a German tongue in English phrases to be transmitted to Vietnamese devotees by unbeliever me was too lofty to attempt. In my humble opinion, bumbling along the eightfold path could generate nothing but contempt for teacher and teaching. We argued. He was incredulous and peeved that I, the Vietnamese, was ignorant of my mother-tongue words which matched concepts in his sermons. I became indignant that a holy man should expect me to produce religious vocabulary.

"I am, ma'am, extremely sorry... I cannot speak Vietnamese."

Above his saffron robe, red blotches bloomed on Master's neck and shiny pate. Was he bemoaning his linguistic limits or apologizing for losing his temper? We parted ways.

The days had grown longer than the nights by the time I got to talk with Soeur *Mỹ Hạnh*. She was a native of *Huế*, capital of Vietnam's last dynasty, the nineteenth century *Nguyễn*. Ten years my senior, *Mỹ Hạnh* moved freely between camps from her order's Roman Catholic convent located in Hong Kong. Her reputation, ardent advocate for many of her people, preceded her. One look at my last formal communication from the Americans, then two years old, was enough to get her started on my case.

It would be weeks before she had word for me. In the meantime, Miss *Linh*, a resident in my hut back in Collinson and neighbour now, shared her happy news that sponsorship by her nephew in Canada was finalized. She vowed to arrange a way out for me. Soeur Mỹ *Hạnh's* investigation concluded I would never get landing privileges anywhere else as long as the USA had me treading water. In other words, if my file remained open on an American desk, no other refugee resettling country would consider an application from me. I wrote *Búp* that if an opportunity in Canada arose, I would jump at it. Coming on three years, I had had enough of waiting. With the nun's help, I withdrew my immigration claim to the land of the free and the home of the brave. I submitted a request for consideration by the true north, strong and free.

Shortly afterwards a UNHCR representative called me in to corroborate the file transfer. His confidence that my case was moving forward renewed my flagging hope. Then my number was announced on a list for transfer to Kai Tak. That refugee transit centre was located in a vintage Royal Air Force site on Victoria Harbour. A hop, skip and a jump from Hong Kong's not-for-the-squeamish runway of the same name, Kai Tak was many a refugee's last stop in Asia. I believed I was among them.

The old base sat on the west side of Kowloon Bay. A bus could deliver us directly from Tuen Mun to Kai Tak so there wasn't another unbearable boat ride for me. Before we boarded, exit processing diverted us to a wicket where I signed for an envelope containing the US$160 held back from my sister's quarterly letters since early 1983. A plastic bag was handed to me too; inside were a grubby pair of pants and a stained shirt pierced by bullet holes. It had been almost thirty-six months since I had last worn that shirt, one thousand one hundred days and counting.

Kai Tak was grungy, but that was no concern to most occupants who came and went quickly. Unlike long-term detainees, no one in transit cared to spruce up the dingy rooms. Minds were set on moving on, not maintenance. The International Committee on Migration posted airline passenger lists two or three times a week. The bulletin board postings brought people running like crazy, flip flops flapping, to scan the outbound ID numbers for their own. What a rush to finally find mine! The Canadian humanitarian quota included me. I dashed off a letter to Miss *Linh* thanking her for her efforts but saying another door had opened. That aerogram took the usual two weeks to travel from Kai Tak to Edmonton, Alberta, Canada.

Then, less than forty-eight hours before my flight, a camp security officer came to the door of my quarters.

He called out, "1243654. Your flight is cancelled."

The flight was not cancelled. Everyone was flying except me. This turn of events hit me like another bullet. It sent me spiralling into profound world-weariness.

"Ahem."

The Buddhist Master had heard about my pending departure. He appeared, wanting to apologize for our earlier misunderstanding. He handed me a comprehensive Vietnamese-English dictionary.

"To help you in your next country."

We spoke of rejection by America and bewilderment at last-minute retraction of travel to Canada. When I mentioned Miss *Linh's* bid to secure me a spot under the umbrella of *Tin Lành*, a Protestant denomination, the monk's temper again got the better of him.

"You know very well," his reprimanding tone rising, "those evangelists are nothing but bad news. You should avoid having anything to do with them." Since the pagoda had never been my spiritual home, I didn't know the Sermon-of-the-Turning-of-the-Wheel-of-the-Law from the Sermon-on-the-Mount. Being Vietnamese did not make me Buddhist. Why had the monk assumed so? Christian charity had been extended; I took help as offered.

I also accepted Master's gift book. Quite ungraciously, I speculated that the dictionary was intended to right the shortcomings of my Vietnamese lexicon vis-à-vis the elimination of self and earthly yen. I had no such desire, nor did I see myself suffering for want of words.

What I lacked was light, the light of understanding, of explanation, and of expectancy. The authorities could have returned me to Tuen Mun but they didn't. Permission to remain in Kai Tak was a good sign. Nevertheless, I lost my appetite and could not sleep. Over the next three months, fatigue and weight loss sapped me. Eventually I learned that direct sponsorship by the Government of Canada had overlapped with a private offer.

True to her word, Miss *Linh* had arranged for a Vietnamese church to submit sponsoring documents on my behalf. Those papers reached some Canadian bureaucrat just in time to scratch me from the DC1 category. Designated Class 1 immigrants were eligible for full government financial assistance. Resettlement funds were reassigned from me to someone else. My file was reclassified as DC3; more time was needed to verify the sponsoring group's resources. That was why my travel documents had been withdrawn in August. Meanwhile the church received informal word that the Government of Canada had taken me under its wing. They pulled back. What could be done?

With chagrin not as deep as desperation, I wrote Miss *Linh* asking that the church resubmit my sponsorship. For this I waited. Worry-fraught and restless, I read and re-read each daily roll of outbound refugees. Week after week, I scanned in vain for Le Thi Hanhtiet. And then...

25 November 1985

From: VHHX

To: YEG

Hanhtiet Le

I lingered long, my fingertip brushing my name. Black ink on white paper. So fragile a promise. So narrow a door.

Three days to go. I bargained with a Vietnamese prep cook in the Kai Tak kitchen; for a price, the Cantonese suppliers could deliver more than menu ingredients. My stomach churned with trepidation.

Two days to go. The sous-chef received my order: slim jeans, an oversized shirt and running shoes. I hadn't been able to bring myself to buy a brassiere from a man and would have to go without. I was coming undone. One day to go. My heart was a yo-yo between ecstasy and agony. Unbelievable happiness at the prospect of release vied with extreme anxiety that some unseen hammer would fall. Leery of uniformed muscle, I shuddered at the sight of Kai Tak police. Would this one or that one block my path?

Wednesday dawned. A cold shower sluiced Asia off my skin. My fingers fumbled at buttons. I couldn't break my fast. Reporting in the yard with two dozen others bound for Canada, Australia and France, I wore a stoic face over a racing pulse and jittery innards. I joined the end of the line snaking onto a bus. No one struck my name from the roster. No one tapped my shoulder or steered me back into detention.

Can you see me there, a skinny bundle of raw nerves behind streaky windows in a bus bouncing up Olympic Avenue to the old Kai Tak Airport Terminal? Freedom had been in my sights for seven seemingly interminable years.

"Is this actually happening? Am I really and truly going to the third country?"

"Already you almost died," I answered myself. "You survived. You endured. You have withstood over three years of soul-battering adversity. For sure, girl, you are going places."

Words which ease the mind, calm the body and soothe the spirit, where is their well?

*S*wimming in Numbers

Clocks talk fluently on both sides of the Pacific. Based on the last one I had read in Hong Kong and the first I saw in Vancouver, Air Canada landed merely three hours after it left. Among the mysteries of jet flight was the sense of motionlessness within the cabin, while without, gravity-slaying speed propelled us through previously irrelevant longitude.

In all my thirty years, I had never traveled faster than fifty kilometres per hour. Bucking the wind as my legs had pedaled a bicycle, my body knew the breeze of resistance. Air currents rushing in through open bus windows tousled hair and left a dousing of dust in their wake. Our escape boat had fought the friction of the ocean and vanquished the pull of the tides. Through the hull I had sensed the reassuring buoyancy that held us afloat, far above seabed trenches. A salty flow had streamed around my fingers and spray broke against a cupped hand dipped over the gunwale. But flying ... no anchor to earth tethered the red-maple-leaf-emblazoned tail of this airborne metal cylinder hurtling some 10,200 kilometres from east Asia to North America's west coast.

My sense of unease only escalated as I contemplated the nothingness on which we were soaring. The pilot announced when we were in the air. That sounded rather stationary. Moving through the air seemed to be more apt, and to carry greater updraft, to me. If we should sink through altitude's transparency, we would shatter into teeny, tiny traces of ourselves. Intuition told me the pressure-controlled cabin was reality but beyond the thin skin of the plane nothing seemed real. Ever diminishing, and farther and farther behind, were all the places I had ever been.

The voice of a steward broke into my wondering, loud and louder. He was the first, but not the last English-speaker to project superiority over me. I felt belittled by his blast. Intensity however, is no substitute for intelligibility. Do people really believe that repeating the very same words at greater volume makes them more meaningful? I was not deaf. Nor dumb. My delay in processing a reply was simply amplified by him adding haughty tone and arrogant attitude into the mix.

Snootiness had worn many faces in my past. Vietnam, isolated in smug victory over the Americans, turned my gaze outward; my sights had been set on a big, open world of open, big-hearted people. Instead, the past three years and three months had been spent within the walls of a world of enclosures, of camps, of confinement. Now, on this incomparable day, I was, like a bird, winging my way freely above and beyond borders. I was neither blind to the human capacity for evil nor naïve enough to believe that ill will was only a local, Asian phenomenon. Anticipating uncountable differences yet to come, I interpreted the steward's condescension as one obstacle among many I would have to surmount. Unable to answer him satisfactorily, I posed an inward, equally unanswerable question, "How often will I have to put up with such people?"

In my imaginings, worry about the future jostled for primary place with fear of falling out of the sky. As my small, known world was receding, an overwhelmingly wide one lay ahead. Like someone myopic edging into a vast, uneven, unfamiliar space, fears of not finding my way, of stumbling, of tripping literally and metaphorically filled me with apprehension. During those twelve uneasy hours enroute, I wished both for the flight to be over and for it to never end.

And then there was longitude. Growing up, I had only known Indochina Time although no one called it that. Time was time – a celestial prerogative unthinkably beyond human manipulation. Hong Kong was sixty minutes ahead of Vietnam, and not just by the single hour of an earlier sunrise. That difference, however, had been imperceptible when sailing in on a slow boat to China. Crossing the International Date Line from Asia to North America, travelers with watches turned them back fourteen hours as the pilot lowered the landing gear in Pacific Standard Time.

While other passengers deplaned, I sat clutching a small plastic carry-on, my only luggage. Outside the airplane, mid-morning Vancouver wore overcast November grey. Immigration officials, accompanied by a thorough translator, met our group of seven from Kai Tak, and declared us Landed Immigrants.

As we moved through the concourse, I gazed into the faces of hundreds of strangers: so many hues, such variety of features, all utterly unlike me. Their mouths moved, and sounds like the chirping of a thousand feasting birds bombarded my ears.

I could scarcely pick out a single comprehensible word. Was this the world in which I would live from now on? How could it be?

Since we had made a safe landing, anxiety about perpetual bafflement began to gnaw at my self-assurance. I felt alertness ebbing. The Intergovernmental Committee on Migration handed each no-longer-a refugee adult a blue and white case with its initials emblazoned on the side and zipped all our documents inside. ICM also distributed light jackets, suitable layering for late autumn on the west coast. One couple and I were guided to a connecting flight. In retrospect, it seemed that no one in British Colombia had a clue what to expect weather-wise in a prairie city in November. Certainly I had no concept of Edmonton in the grip of winter. As our guide left us at the gate for the last leg of our journey, I felt unsteady, unsure.

Brilliant, blinding sunlight above the clouds dimmed as the airplane dipped below them. Early afternoon Alberta was white. A staff member from Catholic Social Services spied us as we passed the gate into the arrivals lounge.

"Where did you come from?" Slow and measured though the question was, we three jetlagged Vietnamese were not thinking in English.

"Hong Kong, yes?"

Only two names were on the gentleman's list. Not mine. This was a danger sign. My name had a history of vanishing from important rosters. Did no one expect me? How careless to whisk a stateless waif half way around the world and strand her in homelessness. I panicked.

"Let's go see," the unruffled fellow said, beckoning us to follow him.

Tired and disoriented, we started down a stairway. A Vietnamese-looking teenager came bounding up two steps at a time.

Speaking our tongue, he blurted out without introduction, "Are you just in from Hong Kong?"

How happy to understand without effort!

"Yes!"

"Are you *Linh's* friend?" the young stranger addressed me. "My aunt is waiting," he gestured below.

This was *Tài,* the nephew whose earlier settlement in Edmonton had enabled his aunt, Miss *Linh,* to resettle here - the event that determined my own journey's end. Beyond revolving doors, I fell into my friend's arms. I felt safe. Someone I knew knew me.

Outdoors, snow was falling. For an instant, my eyes were entranced at the drifting, fragile beauty. Then my muscles tensed and my lungs constricted. It was -30°C. My bright white sneakers slipped. I floundered, stumbling through an unsightly mix of sand, snow, street salt and drippings of antifreeze and engine oil. I avoided looking down. Winter images in magazines and books never touched a nerve like this! All my imaginings of this unknown season had been flawed. Sight had simply failed to transmit the sensations that now wracked my body. Icy air bit my nose and froze bare hands. The cold, raw and bitter, sank its teeth through my inappropriate clothing. What on earth had I done to merit this new cruelty? I had not wanted for pain. Drawing in another bullet-like breath, my lungs exploded, expelling a plume that frosted my hair and my hastily pulled up hood. My life had almost been lost in the flight for freedom. Must I now endure this inconceivable climate? Without warning, the chill of intense disappointment seized and stiffened my dreams. Could weather immobilize wonder?

"I d-d-didn't n-n-kn-ow it was this c-c-cold." My chattering teeth had never been nipped by anything as frosty as that wind. Ice was something I had liked clinking in drinks, crunching cubes a pleasant indulgence.

"Oh, we're in a cold snap today. Normally, the mercury doesn't drop this low."

"How long will this weather last?"

"Til February or March."

"January and February are the coldest."

"Colder than this?"

"You've got that right."

The dismal conversation put me off. I felt in a fog as I followed these friends, entrusting myself to them as knowledge failed and attentiveness faded. Physical exhaustion overtook me when I settled into the back seat of *Tài's* van. The unfamiliar darkness of the early northern dusk sealed me in ignorance of my new city as we drove under overpasses and along thoroughfares dotted with fuzzy amber streetlights glowing through the glass. I turned inward, away from frosty windows which *Tài* had ineffectively scraped.

"Accept it or not," my self-talk began. "You have no choice. You're at the foot of a mountain. Set yourself to learn. Get wisdom."

The twenty-fifth of November, 1985 was a true rebirth for me. I had fancied the fifteenth of August, 1982 as such, but the night I had left Vietnam had, in reality, launched me down a detour, forty months of wondering. Waves of gratefulness washed over me. Words could not express my thanks to all who deserved credit for moving me along the path to where I was that day. So many, many had helped in countless ways. I would forever be in their debt. Exhausted, famished, and floundering in newness to which all around me seemed seasoned, I ate *Linh's* dinner and fell asleep on a bed she had bought for me.

Morning came too soon for my time-zone addled brain. Latitude came into play too. At 53.54°N, my roommates rose in the dark. Day broke after they left for work or school. I was alone. Alone, I surveyed the bedroom crammed with three beds for *Linh*, another woman, *Mỹ*, and me. I untangled myself from the bedsheets and opened the door. Alone, I stepped into the hall. I peered into *Tài's* tiny room. Alone, I tiptoed, unaccustomed to carpet fibers underfoot. *Quang*, *Linh's* older nephew, had left his bedding heaped on the living room sofa. Alone, I gazed at frost flora extravagantly strewn across the window pane. Through the glass, nothing moved. No living being was in sight. I was alone, confined in solitude. My mouth parched with disquiet. In all my life, I had never experienced such isolation.

The phone rang. I jumped.

I could not speak of my feelings. So beholden to *Linh* for bringing me here, tears would choke me if I tried to tell her. And fears, I shrank from acknowledging them. To voice them was too much. Without a soul mate, I had sailed the South China Sea. Without a confidante, I had crossed the Pacific. I needed to find my land legs and step toward independence.

The doorbell buzzed. I started.

My hand quivered as I slid the chain lock in place.

"*Ông tìm ai?*"

"Who are you looking for?"

There was a Vietnamese was on the other side of the door yet it took all my courage to unlock the deadbolt.

"Is your name Le Hanhtiet?"

"Mmm."

Without genteel greetings appropriate for first-time meetings or even a courteous self-introduction, the stranger spoke without panache but of purpose.

"I'm from the Good News Assembly. I'm taking you to apply for Alberta Health Care and Canadian Social Insurance, you know."

I didn't know. Knowing was more precious than gold. Here was an unknown male whose relationship to me wasn't at all apparent. He was trying to get me to go with him to some unfamiliar place. All the alarm bells went off in my head.

Through the slim gap between still-chained door and frame, I studied his face, unable to lipread. "What are those ... ?" I couldn't repeat the English words the stranger had blended into his Vietnamese sentence.

More slowly now, he repeated, "Alberta Health Care? Canadian Social Insurance? I.D."

"Hmm."

I knew my alphabets, Vietnamese and English, and realized abbreviations were ubiquitous but what was I and what did D stand for?

"What's I.D.?"

"Documents that say who you are. Like this."

The man fished out his wallet and showed me a plastic-coated card with a photo that was a reasonable facsimile of his face. "I'm *Phong*, see here," he pointed to his name printed on the card.

Suddenly I recalled *Linh's* letter mentioning a Mr. *Phong* from the sponsoring church. My reluctance ebbed but only slightly. I had been here less than twenty-four hours. Overwhelmed by newness, I longed above all for demystification - clarifications of who, what, where, when, why or how – explanations that signaled some empathy with my unfamiliarity.

I pulled on the windbreaker I had received the day before, slipped on my shoes and unlatched the door. Mr. *Phong* reminded me to bring the ICM case of documents and the apartment key Linh had left for me. Like a child, I trotted after him down the tunnel of a hallway. Every lookalike door was closed. No windows. No people. So quiet. So creepy.

Mr. *Phong* drove me around in a white world. Here an office, there an office, everywhere another office. The provincial health services and the federal revenue agency had my number. I could fall ill and be treated. I could find work and be taxed. With identification, I registered for English language classes. As we rolled through a maze of streets, our sparse conversation turned to education. It seemed that, just as my person wasn't quite real without the stack of new cards bulking up my wallet, so my expertise wouldn't actually exist here without a Canadian diploma or degree. I didn't know the colleges Mr. *Phong* mentioned nor did I see myself ready to requalify in my profession. As valuable as *Phong's* assistance was that morning, he seemed to have no recall of the perplexity of being a new arrival.

When the car stopped, I didn't recognize that we were in the lane behind *Linh's* apartment building. I didn't get out because I had no clue where I was. My Saigon-grown understanding of urban properties was that multi-story residences fronted one roadway only. There, rear walls abutted the back of neighbouring structures which in turn faced only the next street over.

"Here we are," announced *Phong*, "You're home."

"No," I said, shaking my head.

The trash bins and oil-stained parking stalls didn't look like the leafless trees that lined the curb in front of the complex where he had picked me up a few hours earlier. I refused to get out. *Phong* smiled. Without a word of explanation, he shifted out of park. The car juddered up the frozen, rutted alley; we made two right turns and stopped again.

"Is this your place?"

"It looks like it."

"Do you have a key?"

"Yes."

"Can you open the door?"

I could. I did. I got out that car door and through the building entrance. Standing in the vestibule looking up and down the staircases, I froze. Which floor was *Linh's* suite? Which door was her, our, door? I remembered climbing up last night and down this morning so I turned away from the semi-basement. As I was to learn, like most local walk-up apartment blocks, this building had three floors. I trudged up and down every corridor, mounted and descended a couple stairways. Everywhere I saw the same off-white walls, endlessly twisting paisley carpet and identical teak-toned doors which camouflaged dark-tinted metal numerals: 103, 203, or 303. In Saigon, suite numbers had always stood out in contrasting colours above entrances. Lost within metres of home, I was almost in tears when a man entered the hallway.

The resident caretaker watched me. *Linh, Quang, Tài* and *Mỹ* were his only Vietnamese tenants.

He deduced I was the expected fifth occupant and called out, "Looking for your apartment?"

"Yeeesss, sir."

He guided me to one of the mystery doors and pointed out three black figures: 2 0 7.

"Got a key?"

I pulled it out of my pocket. "Yes, sir."

He took it and unlocked the door. As I peered inside, relief washed over me. I recognized *Quang's* mound of blankets on the couch.

"Thank you, sir." I succeeded in keeping my emotions in check.

But outer calm belied inner turmoil. If I got lost, how would anybody find me? If found, how could my finder find my home? That evening, when my new roommates heard about my misadventures, they laughed. With heightened sensitivity to the haplessness of ignorance, my learning curve was going to be stark and steep.

"I came to Canada to rebuild my life," I told myself. "At great risk I escaped Vietnam; there are dangers here too, though different. I must stand on my own two feet. Truly these people have helped me but they are not family. I cannot count on them."

Canada was swimming in numbers. The power and presence of numerals was new; from childhood I had navigated by landmarks. I had no instinct for street, avenue or building coordinates. Address and phone number, along

Hanhtiet, 1985, Edmonton

with roommates' names, and sponsoring church contacts, I wrote up as my own household directory and folded it into my wallet.

The next day impatience pushed me out of the safe zone inside our second-floor suite. Despite the -28°C temperature, I told myself I had a lot to learn and couldn't wait until the others got home after dark. Nervously, I bundled up in layers, borrowed mitts and woolen hat. Through the plate glass door of the building lobby, I stared down the cold. Steeling myself against the climate, I stepped out to the city sidewalk and paused, imprinting the look of our building on my memory. I turned left and walked past other three-story apartment blocks to an intersection. On a street-lamp pole, a narrow green placard labeled 106 ST and, at a right angle, another marked 107 AV. Drivers halted. My courage carried me across the roadway and I continued in the same direction until the next corner where I turned around, shivering. On or beside each building's doors were five figures. Ah! Residences, like residents, required I.D. Those numbers got smaller as I headed for home. After warming up inside, I ventured to the right. I noted 10619, 10613, 10607 and beyond a crossroads 10535, 10529, and so on. Under snow, distinguishing features of construction or landscaping weren't evident; I was baffled by how everyone remembered all the numbers of their many daily destinations.

Later I checked with *Linh*, "I can't find AV in my dictionary. What's AV?"

"How dim can you be? AV means avenue; ST stands for street."

Have you ever felt the weight of what you didn't yet grasp? Not knowing is heavy on the heart; being known for not knowing is oppressive.

The next Sunday I found myself among a great crowd of Vietnamese at the *Hội Thánh Tin Lành Việt Nam.* Since the church had taken on my legal sponsorship, I was indebted to the members although with *Búp* providing every cent of my financial support, I neither expected nor received gifts from the Good News Assembly. I didn't know it then, but the congregation had grown around the nucleus of a few extended families whose three generations had felt their community of faith under fire by the Marxist Commune; they had taken to the sea in search of religious liberty after the south fell to the north. I appeared among them on the first Sunday of Advent and, when my arrival was announced from the pulpit, I stood between the pews and bowed with heart-felt respect to those in front, beside and behind me. Although they had never seen me and did not know me, those assembled had remembered their own statelessness and opened their hearts to bring an unbelieving stranger in. Of all the people I met that December morning, two stood out. Brenda and *Hà* were an interracial couple who approached me and made friendly small talk. They chatted about that Canadian constant which wasn't, the weather. International travelers themselves, they could relate to my jetlag-induced discombobulation. They asked after my sleep habits. My internal clock was still on east Asian time so my sixth day felt like night.

A week or so later, *Hà* and Brenda showed up at our apartment, set a box of food on the counter, and sat down on the sofa for a visit. Fulfilling his role as a liaison between the *Tin*

Lành board and sponsored newcomers, *Hà* had connections at the foodbank. He practiced charity in an unobtrusive way: he used no means test, asked no one to prove they needed the hampers he delivered, and he made no one feel ill at ease about accepting aid.

Encountering unfamiliar food can be awkward. A meal is so much more than a means to filling one's stomach. Bakeries donated bread to the foodbank but the loaves they shared were soft-sided and somewhat squishy. I tried toasting a slice but couldn't swallow the brittle dryness. What bread I had known in Vietnam was a Southeast Asian take on the French baguette. Bread had never been daily fare for me but I associated elasticity and crunch of the crust with complex flavors in each stretchy, sticky, holey bite. The origin of this species of donated loaf was definitely not French. Whoever had packed those hampers also held to the North American belief that dairy was essential, but neither milk nor cheese were customarily on our table. The Vietnamese traditionally fish-rich diet and ubiquitous *nước mắm*, or fish sauce, more than met healthy calcium requirements; tinned milk had been only a treat in *cà phê sửa đá*, dark roast coffee with sweetened condensed milk. Since we rarely ate raw greens – who knew what fertilizer had been used on them or how they had been handled – romaine lettuce joined zucchini and potatoes in a hot pot or soup. Unlike my roommates, I had had some pleasant association with canned food. The cubed peaches and pears, diced pineapple and green grapes of fruit cocktail with a maraschino cherry or two thrown in reminded me of treats from the quartermaster's stock that George had brought home for *Búp*, Dan, Frank and Josie.

After a few weekly deliveries by *Hà*, I suggested the hampers go to someone else in greater need. We were doing all right; everyone in the apartment chipped in a hundred dollars or so a month to cover our grocery and other shared expenses. However, distributing boxes of produce and dry goods wasn't *Hà's* primary purpose. It gave him an in, a way to connect with new arrivals. The material help he graciously offered opened the door for us to trust him with otherwise unvoiced employment, social, and physical or spiritual health needs. Being occupied with meaningful work had kept me on a pretty even keel in the refugee camps but now I had nothing to do, nothing to contribute. *Hà* saw otherwise. He asked if I would like to help others, took me along to the foodbank, and set me up volunteering. There I joined a multi-national crew. Every volunteer had one item to pack; my assignment was often to place potatoes in each cardboard carton. As we carried and emptied sacks or caselots, we didn't chat much. The rhythmic sorting wasn't exciting in the least, in fact, it was boring. However, it got me outside one morning a week, breaking my isolation in the apartment when everyone else was at work. It was a reason to get out into the world and I could walk to the warehouse from our home.

Food. I had known hunger. Here I never saw an empty shelf. My attention was drawn to people who ate even when they were full. Ample supplies bid buyers fill buggies which, at first, I avoided. Try as I might, I couldn't figure out how to unlock one chain-linked to the next. That was only one of my reasons to avoid the big box stores. Grocery warehouses felt factory-like. How could people eat all this food? It was more than extra. It was excessive.

During those first weeks *Hà* invited me to an English conversation circle hosted by none other than *Lai*, the chief thief of Chi Wa Man whose immigration-induced conversion seemed to have stuck. Here he was a most genial host, plying up to a dozen Vietnamese with tastes of home. We sat on the furniture-less carpeted floor as Deborah, a young Canadian woman, tried to keep a choppy English dialogue going. I found her questions very simple but the answers less so. While "What did you do last week?" was completely comprehensible, I hadn't done anything – at least not anything worth talking about. I could have said, "Nothing" but that would have made me sound witless or, even worse, sassy. Several of the others couldn't explain themselves in English and reverted to Vietnamese. Hearing their northern accents flipped a critical switch inside of me; I was reluctant to engage with questionable characters. For my whole life, the *Hanoi* accent had been associated with enmity and combativeness. My thoughts wandered above the Vietnamese hum. My mind associated the sting of spending years behind bars or barbed wire with their ilk, with the pain of losing my country, and the sadness of separation from my sister and her children. My heart had been set on Canada freeing me from all of that, but in an absurd twist of fate I was among northerners again. What was I doing sitting and eating with these strangers?

The conversation moved on without me. A few of the men, more fluent in English, launched into seriously exhaustive accounts of suffering under re-education or harrowing escapes. They sensed in Deborah a compassionate listener and began to divulge memories long-repressed. After another session or two, I concluded that several of the men, for there were only a couple women participating, were out to acquire a girlfriend, preferably Canadian, or to engineer sponsorship arrangements for family members scattered around the globe in precarious situations. Language acquisition wasn't their priority at all. I saw no English, no order and no point in attending. The hearts of the Canadians involved were noble so I didn't, indeed couldn't, critique the service they were offering. I just chose not to return.

Nevertheless, I resolved to keep my ears and eyes open. Learning through listening was essential, and perceiving through sight seemed elemental, but speaking seemed secondary until I left the safety of a majority Viet milieu. *Linh* and *Mỹ* took me shopping at a vast, indoor market called the Kingsway Garden Mall where I found neither a king nor a garden. Inside McDonald's, all three of us gazed silently at the wall-mounted menu, glowing but bewildering. The girls insisted I order for us. What did they want? As we struggled to read, interpret and make a choice, the queue in the rapid service line inched ever closer to the cashiers.

"I like those skinny, yellow-ish sticks," said *Mỹ*.

But none of us could name French fries.

"Next please" meant us. We shuffled over still uncertain. Customers waited behind us. The cashier waited before us. The weight of their thinning poise flustered me. I panicked.

"Three coca cola," I said just because I could say that and be understood.

My roommates' indignation should have been balanced by their ignorance of how to negotiate a fast food purchase, but it wasn't.

As our huffiness subsided, I recognized the gnarly fear of judgment twisting our relationship. We worried that Canadians would find us foolish or even tell us to "go back home." Next time at the food court, we decided, we would copy exactly what the person ahead of us had done. However, in the din of the order counter, we couldn't hear what was said. We resorted to squinting at the menu.

"Top," I said, pointing. "First one, second one, third one."

Our tray held a Big Mac, a ¼ pounder with cheese, and a ¼ pounder. By this method, we eventually worked our way through the entire menu trying new items we had never tasted before, and often chose never to order again. Like *Mỹ*, I preferred fries. Hot. Crispy. With tomato ketchup.

The mall's boutiques were pricier than the massive department stores with racks and racks of unattended inventory organized by size. S stood for small. P also meant small. Both P and S were sometimes big enough for a Vietnamese woman to swim in. Passing around carousels stuffed with full-length coats, I squatted down and disappeared from view in a forest of down, faux fur, and polyester gabardine. A winter parka was to be my first purchase. Perhaps it was the dizziness from zipping up and down so many jackets, or the headiness of a myriad choices but when my friends called me to go, I turned and walked towards *Linh's* reflection smack into a floor-to-ceiling mirror. What you see isn't always what you get.

Donna, one of the church founders' granddaughters, *Linh*, and I accepted Deborah's invitation to a Christmas event presented by an English-speaking church. Deborah's father, Mister Rudy, picked us up along with several others who crammed into his sedan. The windshield and windows steamed up as we breathed warmth against the cold night. Mister Rudy rolled down his window to ventilate the car. From my vantage point in the backseat, I could see how he took the wintery blast, squeezed against the driver's door by the 3 passengers on the front bench. His kind voice invited each of us to introduce ourselves but Donna answered for all. The ride to and from the program was a hoot. Our laughter and giddiness enroute were more memorable than the pageant itself which lacked the innuendo and farce of Vietnamese melodrama. Whether he knew it or not, Mister Rudy, like *Hà*, in his enthusiastic bigheartedness, was doing a great service to newcomers and the society which had swallowed us whole. Many recently arrived Vietnamese, despondent in the dark winter months, rarely stepped out of doors. In one walk-up apartment or another, I noted neighbors gambled and drank with other Vietnamese-speakers, dousing, never quite drowning, their migrant miseries in adrenalin or alcohol. Drawing us with kindness out of the bleak familiar widened our horizons which, even without words, spoke promise of better things to come.

My neighbourhood explorations continued. Within a couple weeks, I received word that an orientation class for new arrivals was set to begin. With *Linh's* help, I plotted the route from our place to the Mennonite Centre for Newcomers just four blocks away.

MCN was the response of congregations of earlier European settlers, themselves displaced by revolution or the world wars, to refugees in the 1970s and 80s. A founding member, Miss Anne Falk, had roots in the peace and reconciliation mission of the Mennonite Central Committee in South Vietnam before 1975. She and Mr. *Thành* welcomed me to my first class in December 1985.

What a contrast to the other people, almost entirely Vietnamese, whom I had encountered to date! Mr. *Thành's* frank lessons made an indelible impression. The curricula seemed to respond to the very questions of my mind and address the insecurity in my soul. Secrets of this new country were unwrapped and interpreted each and every day. His keen sensitivity to the bafflement of all things new was matched by his awareness that when ignorance was laughed at, learning was stifled while fear flourished.

"No one knows everything. Long term residents aren't better than you."

He explained that experience had been his best teacher. Never overlooking details, Mr. *Thành* illuminated the mysteries of the mundane. For instance, the fine shirt he was wearing would cost us fifteen dollars new at the Kingsway Garden Mall; however, he revealed that he had bought it for just two. How? Shop second-hand. And in those cavernous indoor retail spaces, we dared not think the merchandise was untended. Department and big box stores had none of the human contact we had known all our lives in the little shops or market stalls where proprietors had greeted us, often by name. Here however, cameras and plain-clothed security were watching. Shoplifting would be a blot on our personal record and on the entire Vietnamese community.

Clothing was a concern. None of us knew how to dress for the weather. Gone were the dry and rainy seasons and one wardrobe that suited both. We learned of four seasons and that related fashions weren't primarily about appearance. Thick boots and padded overcoats made even the limber lumber but being warm had little to do with looking hot. In spring, which Mr. *Thành* repeatedly assured us would come, lighter weight clothes ought to protect against falling rain and slush or mud splashing up. Summer, the closest climatically to what we had grown up with, was going to last only two or three months. In Edmonton, the weather could change on a dime so even in July or August one had best be prepared for wind, wet or worse. Autumn, as picturesque as illustrations in classic elementary readers, meant cool winds that stripped trees. The leafless elms along inner city boulevards were not dead or defoliated by agent orange. Green just wasn't part of their mid-winter garb.

Our cluster of newcomers role-played telephone calls, trying out gambits and greetings.

"Please hold" didn't mean I should grip the receiver any tighter.

"See you later" was an appropriate way to sign off even though our ears, not our eyes, had met.

"Who's calling, please?" was a culturally upscale version of "Who are you?" And "I am Anne" sounded gauche to Canadians accustomed to "This is Anne speaking."

Vietnamese restauranteurs established since 1978 were leasing space north of Edmonton's downtown rail yards. The menus boasted everything from *phở* to *bánh mì*. A Vietnamese sub was not the equivalent of a Canadian sandwich. We shouldn't expect layers of sliced meats, cilantro, slivered carrot and slices of potent chili in every shop with the word submarine on its menu.

Literal translations were particularly dubious when it came to medical lingo. Many of our practice phone dialogues were about setting up appointments and describing ailments even though there was a Vietnamese physician in family practice within walking distance. He would soon be hearing our aches and pains.

Meanwhile, Miss Anne began taking me along on hospital visits. Although she had spent a couple of years in South Vietnam, she hadn't mastered the five tones in our language let alone the seven of the northern dialect. Hospitalized Vietnamese were not very tolerant of muddled accents but between my ear, our shared medical backgrounds and Anne's fluent English, we collaboratively translated various women's health matters.

Those first weeks learning and laughing *with* others equally disoriented made a world of difference to me. I was not alone. My classmates were also struggling to get their bearings. Our teacher truly welcomed us. I had met an honourable and trustworthy person on whom I could call with any question. Mr. *Thành* sowed seeds of hope. A way had opened before me. I could walk in it.

Tail Lights

Driving lessons were high on *Búp's* list of priorities for me. I took her long distance advice with a grain of salt. My sister was calling from California. My recollection of her behind the wheel of George's parked car was the closest I could come to picturing her as a driver. In the decade since she had settled in greater L.A., *Búp* had graduated from driveway to expressway. She may have seen an icy street in Kansas, but had never operated a car on a wintry road in Canada.

"The snow is slippery. The streets are dangerous. I don't think this is the right time."

"You've got to get out. Get moving and get on with your life. Don't sink into dependence."

But dependent I was. *Búp* had sent two thousand dollars for *Linh* to forward to the church as a deposit guaranteeing sponsorship. Under a private charity, I was not eligible for full government financial aid. Once I had opened a bank account, a government allowance for refugee students of $350 per month enabled me to cover my share of the rent, groceries, and telephone bill. That was also enough to purchase basic toiletries, some stationery, and a bus pass. I was becoming comfortably mobile on the city transit system and did not envy *Quang* his brand-new car.

My mind was set on learning, not yearning for stuff. Before my first full-time English class wound down that summer, I realized my language skills still fell far short of the professional standard required for nursing. Thanks to the guidance of Elaine, a most remarkable teacher whose effectiveness in the classroom was exceeded only by her mothering heart, I enrolled in another twenty weeks of English language learning.

Confidence, not vocabulary or grammar, was my biggest deficit. The five-hour-a-day classes at Alberta Vocational Centre were my first exposure to an eclectic mix of international accents. I knew mine was different; I was the only Vietnamese in the advanced class among speakers of Spanish, Polish, Khmer, Tigrinya, Korean, French and Amharic. During my six years of secondary school English learning, I had read, written and listened to, but never spoken the English language and was timid about making mistakes. Vietnamese has no blended consonants such as bl or pr. If I chatted about preparing dinner, listeners heard "repairing" dinner and guessed something had gone wrong in the kitchen. Stressing the wrong part of a four or five syllable word confused my classmates. On paper, educate, educator, and education looked related but lengthening DU or TION rather than ED or CA muddled the message. When I explained my nursing "e-DU-ca-tion", it sounded like "Had you question?" Copying my Québécois classmate's "educaTION" didn't improve matters. Describing an "en-GINE" rather than an "EN-gine" perplexed a Peruvian medic seated beside me; he wondered what angina had to do with our assignment to compare and contrast cars and buses.

The mature women and men I studied with made great allowances and adjustments for each other; my reticence to speak decreased in the presence of classmates whose visible differences were irrelevant. In heart and mind, they were just like me. Our instructor's ability to understand everyone almost all the time amazed me. The atmosphere of acceptance and accommodation bolstered my self-assurance. Face-to-face conversations where misspeaking was a springboard to learning and not to scorn were invaluable. From my point of view on the fringes of Canadian society, I couldn't be a member of the community without the language.

Elaine noticed my diligence in the multi-level class and gave supplementary activities for me to do on my own. She fostered the spirit of learning; I could not adequately express my gratitude for her professional manner and devotion to her students. Even more than I was, I saw many learners weighed down with cares: children acting out in this much more permissive society; loss of status; relatives missing in war zones; predatory salesmen; exploitative bosses often within their own cultural communities; marriages crumbling; debts mounting. We didn't carry on friendships outside of school. After dismissal, everyone huddled in bus shelters before making our separate ways to shuffle children home on transit, or pick up shift-work, earning minimum wage or less to meet family obligations, repay debts, or keep promises so that, when we did lie down, we could hope to sleep.

I was living on the edge financially but didn't want *Búp* to worry. Classmates working evening janitorial jobs gave me a heads-up about an opening. From five to nine p.m., I emptied waste paper bins, vacuumed, scrubbed toilets and mopped floors for four dollars an hour. Alberta's capital had plenty of vacant commercial real estate in 1986. Five years after the New Energy Policy, bankruptcies were declining but brakes remained on the oil industry.

Professionals in suits and heels were leaving their cushy jobs as I traveled up the elevator to the twenty-second floor of an office tower every weekday. From the plate glass windows, I could see streams of red tail lights flowing out of the downtown. The green-banked curves of the North Saskatchewan River wound southwest and northeast. After the bleak months of my first winter, nature's revival comforted me. I felt tranquility from my bird's eye view on such beauty.

Though my eyes drank in the green panorama, my heart was not above the tree tops. And those trees, small from my skyscraper perch, seemed scarcely taller when I walked beneath them, slender and lean, utterly unlike the towering trunks and ample boughs of *Đồng Nai*. Here the wind blew dry and stiff. It spoke in unfamiliar tones, howling sometimes around the angular, unnaturally altered cityscape. The prairie breeze rarely carried the scents of blossoms and never bore the fragrance of tropical fruit on air so humid it had rooted us to Earth.

Leafy neighbourhoods stretched toward the horizon and on long June evenings the street lights hadn't even turned on as I walked ten blocks home. As a petite woman passing through the Rathole, a vehicle and pedestrian tunnel under the railyards that separated the city centre from blocks and blocks of walk-ups, I was blissfully unaware of urban dangers. Naïve, innocent really, I felt Canadians were good people. During those days, nothing shattered my belief that I could

trust everybody. The freedom to walk at dusk without threat
or harm was another dimension of the new, open life I reveled
in after three complicated years of compressed mobility,
controlled activity, and compact space in refugee camps.

On the nineteenth floor of the Metropolitan, the cleaner
was an elderly woman whose accent hobbled her Vietnamese.
Like many women in the Chinese diaspora, Mrs. Lam had
lived within a self-sufficient community. In her case, growing
up and beginning a family in *Cholon*, the predominantly
Cantonese district around Saigon's *Chợ Rẫy* Hospital, she
hadn't required fluency in Vietnamese. For the most part I
could understand her. Our Polish supervisor wanted me to do
the heaviest tasks on Mrs. Lam's floor. Mrs. Lam learned I came
straight to work from school. She mothered and mentored me.
Although she barely spoke English, she had found work and
did it diligently. During the day on her senior's transit pass,
she explored the city by bus. Few young people had the guts
to go alone and do as she did. Mrs. Lam's spirit inspired me.
She became my teacher, exemplifying how we need each other
– that we social beings are only as rich as our relationships.
From time to time her husband exasperated her or her son
annoyed her but Mrs. Lam never whined. Commenting once
about a tiff and tossing it forever off the table with a joke or a
chuckle, she was quick-witted. We shared many a laugh. Mrs.
Lam almost always brought a sandwich or cold dish to share
with me. Her generosity, on a wage no better than mine, made
me uncomfortable. I tried to refuse.

"Eat. You no eat, you no vacuum. You no vacuum, I no job."

I ate. I vacuumed. I studied. I prepared a resume to work
as a health care aide. I never heard back from a single one

of my first dozen applications. In 1986, it wasn't easy to find work in Alberta. For all the puffery about equal opportunity and the merits of skill, getting my foot in the door depended largely on knowing someone with pull. I didn't.

One person who had known me from birth had been but a voice on the phone for eight months following my resettlement in Canada. Finally, when winter's chill was off and summer vacation freed my sister from prodding her Americanized teenagers out of bed and off to school, *Búp* flew up from California. Our first face-to-face meeting in eleven years was, and remains, a reverie.

The sinews of sisterhood, in our case, sweet and strong, had been stretched and almost severed by the socialist republicans of Vietnam. After *Búp* and the children were evacuated along with George in April, 1975, she had vanished from my view. *Búp* and other Vietnamese scrambling to adapt to American ways in America correctly read how the newly dominant northern regime handled "propaganda" from the lair of their enemy. State-side *Việt Kiều* communication sent to relatives in the south branded us there as traitors. Nevertheless, anxiety about our well-being overrode complete caution. Since *Búp* hadn't known where she would land before our sudden separation, I knew nothing of her destination but the vast U.S. of A. My sister thought she knew where I was. She never imagined the post-war turmoil that had turned me out of her familiar, former apartment. A few of *Búp's* letters that first year eventually returned "undeliverable" to Hawthorne, California. Others disappeared, probably under the scissors of postal censors. *Búp* panicked. With faint hope, she wrote a few lines to a former neighbour mercifully still at a Saigon address *Búp* remembered. This woman, herself the mother of an Amerasian, understood that nosy eyes and ears were everywhere. She sent a young man to *Chợ Rẫy* hospital with an innocuous invitation for me. That "drop in sometime" message compelled me to pedal into the *Bàn Cờ* neighbourhood at shift end. Since the envelope from *Búp* had been addressed to Mrs. *Nhiển*, she had opened it. The letter inside was spare in details, but *Búp's* address was noteworthy; it had re-established a tenuous link between us in 1976.

For the next six years in that pre-digital age, we had exchanged lean letters two or three times annually. What was there for intensely private people to tell when sticky seals were routinely pried open by public officials? Grandmother's death was shareable but I never breathed a word about how I had come to be homeless. As long as I was employed at the hospital, I could say so. Mother's health and mine were worth mention. I always asked after the children and George. My sister's replies about Dan, Frank, and Josie reassured me but she never, ever commented on her marriage. Her husband seemed out of the picture. I tried to put two and two together; was something amiss? The *Chợ Rẫy* postal kiosk clerk, a pre-liberation acquaintance, always passed along aerograms from America without question until she was replaced by a northerner.

"Even now," not so subtly gloating over Vietnam's perceived drubbing of the USA, the new clerk's feigned surprise dripped with accusation. "You receive letters from loser Americans?"

I became extremely uneasy. That was the first time I had been confronted in such a manner.

"This is from my sister," I replied as politely as possible.

Blood being thicker than water, no amount of brain-washing was likely to rid me of the stain of an imperialist-sympathizing sibling. Not that the authorities didn't try. Grilling, drilling for evidence of espionage, had begun.

I considered using a return address other than the hospital. The delivery of international mail out to Mother's rural district would have raised more suspicions than in the city. Asking a friend for postal privileges was out of the question. I wouldn't put anyone else at risk.

Back then I had despaired of ever seeing my sister again. But here, by a long and circuitous route, we stood together in the chill of an airport arrivals lounge, heart to heart, holding, clinging to each other.

The next six days were too short to fill in all the gaps in all the letters and all the innuendoes in the recent phone conversations easily overheard by *Búp's* family or my roommates. Thankfully it was July. We walked and walked beyond earshot, and talked and talked of hurts long hidden and sorrows suppressed. Sharing tears with a sympathetic ear, we sensed how each had often cried alone. What tough days my sister had had settling into a strange place. She had had three spirited small kids, hardly any education, no independent means, and inter-spousal misunderstandings with insufficient words or will to find a way. The mountain she had climbed was not gold, but with tenacity and intelligence, she had secured gainful, profitable employment. Working harder and longer at soldering circuit boards than she'd ever had to do, even in Saigon's servant underclass, *Búp* had pushed her limits to save and send what she could to sustain our mother and me. Those parcels of pharmaceuticals or fabric for Mother to use, or for me to sell, had been sealed and unwrapped in infinitely more valuable hope. Recalling those days and unpacking the meaning together with my sister put present struggles into perspective.

One of my trials was to keep chipping away at the barriers to the nursing profession. The Canadian health system was a mystery. I found my way to the United Nurses of Alberta and asked face to face about writing a challenge exam. This was not an option. Apparently to establish my credentials or assess my skills, nothing short of a college transcript would do. As persona non grata in *Hồ Chí Minh* City, it was impossible for me to secure the required documents from the Institute of Nursing. Although Canada had re-established diplomatic relations broken off with Vietnam in 1975, there would be no embassy in Hanoi until 1994 and no consulate in the former Saigon for another three years after that. Nursing, by definition, was caring for people. In Canada, it seemed caring about paper took precedence over people.

Mr. *Thành*, a continuing source of wisdom, recommended I learn from the inside by volunteering. So began a three month stint at the General Hospital. Three times a week I assisted with feeding in a long-term care unit. This experience opened my eyes to the North American cultural practice of institutionalizing the elderly infirm, a concept entirely foreign to me. My nursing experience had been limited to acute care in Vietnam. Our elders grew old in the homes of their children with grandchildren and even great grandchildren forming multi-generational households.

Thrust into a throng of debilitated pensioners all isolated from their families, I was distressed by a pervasive melancholy. I had never seen a gathering of so many seniors as the one in the dining room that first day. All looked immobile and seemed utterly dependent on strangers. Later I met the odd family member who occasionally came to sit with an aged parent or grandparent through a meal and assist with feeding. I knew no Canadian families. I knew nothing of the geographic distances that separated generations even within one city. Clock-bound shifts and rigid timetables in this mechanized, industrial society were a far cry from the more supple work schedules of farmers or mom-and-pop shop keepers in Vietnam.

I reckoned I had no option but to adjust to and accept this alien culture. The Canadian lifespan was longer than that of the average Vietnamese. Did people live longer by mustering the aged into silent, shuffling masses? What dignity was theirs? My heart sank as I watched the flickering light of the television screen reflected in the eyeglasses of the elders wheeled into place before it. Being a mealtime volunteer, I was not invited past the queue of wheelchairs into the private rooms. I felt there was a wall through which I was not permitted to pass.

As a volunteer, I felt marginalized by nursing staff. Few were open to conversations. Perhaps they considered confidentiality a concern but they came across as cold. Maybe they couldn't understand my speech. I was indeed very self-conscious about being incomprehensible. The intimacy with study and work mates I had known and now missed amplified the remoteness I sensed here. Social and emotional tenderness of these nurses and aides may have been reserved for other activities at other times of day. Initial impressions though confirmed how guarded most Canadians were of their personal space and private perspectives. I never witnessed there, nor experienced, a meeting of minds.

There were other relationships to build. My sister wanted me to journey to Hawthorne to get reacquainted with her children and George. The American Consulate in Calgary was the closest source of the proper documents for a landed immigrant like me. Getting there depended on the good graces of *Hà* and Brenda who had befriended me months before. This was my first foray outside the city since my landing. Dim twilight vistas from my backseat viewpoint faded to black as we headed south.

Brenda's parents were going to host us overnight. Other than a class visit to Elaine's farm, the Carletons were the first Canadians to invite me into their home. All along the 280 kilometre car ride, apprehension about staying with strangers riddled me. How was I to behave? When should forks and knives be used at the table? If I couldn't recognize the ingredients, would I be able to swallow the food? What if my stomach wouldn't cooperate with social niceties? Would I give the right answers? Might I say the wrong thing? Misgivings about misplacing metaphors and uncertainty about interpreting comments or gestures never waned. Decades later, this lack of communicative confidence lingers. In my adult-learned language, I could never rid myself of feeling short on verbal poise. The new tongue just wasn't mine.

The novelty of that trip was almost obliterated by the shake-up waiting back in Edmonton. As I unlocked our apartment door, *Quang* called out.

"Who's there?"

"It's just me."

"You can enter."

Gone was the jungle of house plants that used to line the living room window. There had been a family squabble. *Linh* had tried to assert parental powers over almost adult *Tài*. As a result of the clash, the brothers and aunt agreed to separate. In what had been the girls' bedroom, my clothes and other belongings were stuffed into big green garbage bags. A note from *Linh* said she had done the packing. Obviously I wasn't staying.

Quang confirmed that *Linh* had already moved two beds to a suite seven blocks away. In fact those box springs and mattresses were the only furnishings *Linh* and *Mỹ* had in the new apartment when I reached it. I couldn't afford to live alone so I fetched my bags to set up housekeeping with them in the echoey rooms. We had no dishes, cooking utensils, no shower curtain or phone. I had no bed. My very first major purchase was at a flea market where I bought a second-hand one for thirty bucks. A member of our sponsoring church trucked it home for me. Once word was out about our dilemma, gifts started arriving: one oak dining chair, two more with chrome legs and vivid emerald and lemon vinyl seats, plus a stool upholstered in tropical orange. Someone else donated a table.

We received a TV console and a TV. The television was highly entertaining in part because of its faulty components. If anyone walked past it with a particularly heavy foot, the sound might fail. Some evenings we lounged on our saggy, previously owned sofa and made up Vietnamese dialogues to accompany the announcers or actors on screen. When static snow replaced the video feed, we turned to improv, gesticulating accompaniment to the disembodied voices of the nightly CTV news anchors whose mannerisms we came to know better than those of any other Canadian. With my next paycheque, we bought a VCR. Kung Fu flicks were in our blood. Movie series out of Hong Kong or Taipei with up to a dozen prequels or sequels could be rented down the block. On Fridays after grocery shopping, we whipped up some supper and watched videos until perhaps five or six in the morning.

The allure of the screen was not simplistic escapism. Rather than dodging reality, fiction animated actual disputes we could not talk about. We were not all the same, all of us lumped together under labels such as newcomers, refugees, Southeast Asians, or Vietnamese. In ever narrower categories right down to three, single, young, female roommates, our individual experiences and our diverse perspectives on those happenings easily jeopardized harmony. To a great degree, our generation had been raised on ancient Confucian foundations. Social mores were intended to keep relationships in regulated balance. There was tension with Taoist spontaneity. Free expression turned out to be far from ideal for society. Not being hermits, somebody's liberty to swing her arm sooner or later struck someone else as wrong. Feuding families, jilted lovers, excommunicated believers, exiled refugees, we had all been wronged. However, we lacked mechanisms to work through, and work out, our differences. Skillful film-makers presented a unity in diversity that our lives lacked. And so we roared approval at the exploits of our favourite actors and crashed with their calamities. When I worked evenings, I often arrived home to find *Linh's* eyes red-rimmed and swollen. Even her upper lip looked puffy. From dusk to dawn she had been weeping over the tragedies of truly kickass martial arts heroines.

Film fiction aside, *Linh*, *Mỹ* and I lived lightheartedly. We owned little and owed nothing, paying always in cash; no debts, no worries. I felt truly liberated, traveling through life without luggage. Although my two roommates participated in the congregation of the Vietnamese Alliance Church, holy writ against fretting, or in favour of thankfulness, didn't instinctively infiltrate thinking there. Seekers of the kingdom of heaven, of course, were not immune to earthly acquisitiveness, so our happy simplicity didn't go unnoticed. Many members dropped in, curious about our contentment. If it was meal time, we simply pulled up another mismatched chair and shared. Food was a comfort. Increasingly authentic ingredients were available for Vietnamese cuisine in local shops; my tongue became adept at sensing and sourcing elementary flavouring. While the purchase of ever newer and grander houses possessed many of our acquaintances, we made them feel at home with aromas and tastes that had traveled ten thousand kilometres. I did not consume beyond my means and ate with gratitude.

Alongside every choice, consciousness of freedom from either obligation or tyranny danced with unpretentious elegance. Unlike those days in Camp Collinson when the present had no cares but an unknown future gnawed at carefreeness, I knew now to savour the moment. This living lightly and joyfully was not something I observed among publicly religious people. No seasoned believers ever drew me into their intimate circles. Family groups were tight, even exclusive. If, in private piety, brotherly love exceeded ostentatious glitz and glamour I did not know. I couldn't glimpse God in those who claimed to be made in his image. An abundant life, I figured, was about more than posing with the latest model car in front of the widest garage. I was moving forward in hope. Economy enabled liberality.

Less may mean more. *Linh* was less of a cook than I was. She was usually content to scour woks and scrub pots so we were quite surprised to find her preparing supper one evening. Like the film stars in her favorite musicals, *Linh* turned everyday banter into a tune.

Someone, just an ordinary someone,

Now an angel in your kitchen,

Like magic makes a meal

That satisfies your body and your soul.

Mỹ and I burst out hooting at *Linh's* impromptu lyrics. We also teased her about her less than magical culinary skills.

At another time, *Linh's* off-key antics got the better of *Mỹ*. Claiming she had tired of such singing, *Mỹ* bought a tape player and retreated to her bedroom with her stash of cassettes. *Linh* and I lurked, ears against our room-mate's door. We couldn't resist another dig.

Someone, just an ordinary someone,

Now self-exiled in her bedroom,

Rich music without friends

Makes melodies morose and roommates cry.

Mỹ good-naturedly relented and responded to our poking by setting up her stereo next to the dining table.

The give and take of my friends' daily lives was very different from mine. *Mỹ's* world was almost entirely Vietnamese. From work at the garment factory to conversations with her fiancé, she negotiated her world in our mother tongue. *Linh* had started out doing detailed auto cleaning. The fumes nauseated her so much that she often sat at the supper table unable to eat. Washing cars was a bitter pill to swallow for a young woman who had enjoyed expensed trips to trade shows in *Hanoi* promoting products of the central provinces. After a couple years as a sewing machine operator, *Linh* moved on to dental lab training where her only daily interactions were with the Canadian boss.

I observed diversity among boat people. Those in our community whose flight had been fueled by fearful state harassment and smothering police surveillance identified more quickly with, and integrated more deeply into, Canadian society. Unlike purely economic migrants, for us there was no going back. I could not and did not indulge in ruminations of the good old days. The past was the past, although after-effects lingered. Years of being black-listed made me guarded and reticent to meddle. What people told me unprompted I kept to myself. I eschewed prattle; I would not pry. And yet Canadian doors didn't open without someone applying persuasive pressure.

On My Own Two Feet

When it came to job-hunting, opportunity wasn't knocking, so I had to. Scouring the telephone directory, not just the paltry classified ads, I found the Good Samaritan Auxiliary Hospital. At the end of an hour long bus ride, I arrived at a facility for the aged established three decades earlier by charitable Lutherans. I had no one particular to ask for. Just as I was handing my resume to the receptionist, the director's assistant walked by.

"I'm looking for work. I have emergency room experience in Vietnam."

The Good Samaritan graciously received my application that day, and phoned soon after to set up a formal discussion. Teacher *Thành's* course almost two years earlier had just touched on job interviews. However, like countless immigrants from cultures in which strangers are never hired on the strength of a self-promoting conversation, I had never had to sell myself to a potential employer. Without a strategy, I simply answered the many questions of the two interviewers. Marjorie, the assistant director, seemed genuinely interested in both my professional background and refugee experience. I had no inkling then of the links she had immediately made between local Lutheran donors whose philanthropy extended beyond church-initiated health care in Edmonton to World Relief in Hong Kong camps.

Acknowledging my unaccreditable acute-care skills and what was deemed adequate English, I was hired as a casual health care aide on day shifts. It never occurred to me that working as an aide was beneath me. I had met people so puffed up by advanced degrees that they couldn't put their hand to any practical task. Theory is comeliest in application. Shoulder to the wheel, I determined to repay my employer for taking a chance on me. I switched my continuing education studies from day to evening and didn't drop my English classes. Communicating with hard-of-hearing residents who strained to recognize some of my words motivated me to keep improving my speech. The Canadian nursing staff came in a range of sizes, all taller and wider than I was. Uniforms came in large, medium and petite. The suppliers needed to add another, smaller, Southeast Asian.

Initially I was the only Vietnamese at the Good Sam. There was so much to learn from my new colleagues whose Swedish, German, Dutch, Polish, Ukrainian, Indian and Filipina roots and interpretations both confounded and enriched me. Observing many cultures mixing in the workplace, I absorbed countless unsought lessons. For instance, my workplace was home to mostly elderly residents. Home is hardly just one's sleeping space and may well be our dearest antithesis to all things institutional. Being at home means saying 'no' to cubed cherry jello and 'yes' to borscht and buttered white rolls. Food preferences formed at family tables before or during the First World War had implications for the health of the ladies and gentlemen I fed, dressed, and wheeled around in the late 1980s. To cheer them, encourage them, and stimulate them by conversation, I had to enunciate well. Naturally reticent to speak up when uncertain about words or grammar, I had no choice but to push past my inhibitions. Every day embedded me deeper into the wider English world beyond my own ethnicity. Through daily exposure to elders whose diverse origins and paths through the Great Depression and World War II made them treasured teachers, I realized there was never enough of that kind of learning.

Although I was small, my colleagues saw I wasn't lazy. I knew how to transfer long-term patients safely from bed to wheel-chair. Being eager to learn and pleasant with everyone was how I made my mark. In those days, the Good Sam wasn't merely where we worked. It was who we were. The nursing staff drew outsiders in. Although I didn't fully appreciate it then, the mutual loyalty and cooperative care for residents and for each other would outlast career changes, retirements and our own aging. Those with seniority modeled and made way for newcomers like me to stand on my own two feet, carrying my share of the load, not stepping on others' toes. No one expected that work had to be fun to be good. It was good work that made shared shifts fun. Within three months, I was offered a part-time position with benefits. I began picking up extra shifts; indeed, I was scared to say no whenever phoned to fill a vacancy. Sometimes I worked a hundred hours in two weeks. The scheduler and I had to have a chat about exceeding fulltime limits and tax implications of so much overtime.

By penny-pinching, I set aside enough to pay for summer driving lessons. After more scrimping and saving, I bought a car for sixteen hundred dollars. Other than new tires, I spent nothing on upgrades. My roommates teased me about being so cheap that the 1968 Pontiac hatchback didn't even have a radio.

I laughed.

"Hey! We've been walking, now we're rolling. As for rocking, we know how to make music!"

And so our trio warbled to the green grocers, the duck roasters and the whole-food butchers. On weekends, we crooned together under moonlight, going and coming much later than any of us would have walked alone in the inner city.

Driving did not cure me of my dependance on landmarks but made me more appreciative of city planning. The wisdom of numerically ordered streets and avenues wasn't apparent to the directionally challenged. Once, out-of-town Vietnamese guests phoned to say they had arrived.

"We're at 7-11," they announced. "Tell us how to get to your place."

"Where are you exactly?"

"At 7-11."

"Yes, tell me precisely where."

"At the payphone at 7-11."

"No, which 7-11?"

"Which 7-11?"

"Yes, which 7-11? There are several 7-11s."

"Hmm. How can I tell which 7-11 I'm at?"

"Are you near an intersection?"

"Yes. We're at the 7-11 near the intersection with traffic lights."

There was no point in pointing out the city had 847 signal-controlled intersections.

"Okay. Look on the street posts near those traffic lights. Do you see small green placards with white numbers?"

"Uhh...it's too far to see."

"Get your son to run to the corner and report back on two sets of numbers: numerals before AV and before ST."

"My son is sleeping in the car."

"I see. Well, either walk to the intersection yourself or go into the 7-11 and ask the clerk for the avenue and street of this intersection."

"Couldn't you just come and meet me here and show me the way to your place?"

They weren't the only ones at sea in the city.

My car reduced travel time to and from work to just fifteen minutes. I stuck to one unchanging route that got me there reliably rain or shine. By driving, I gained an hour and a half each day to study which I did after my usual three to eleven p.m. shifts. If I turned out the lights by two, I could still squeeze in five or six hours of sleep before morning upgrading classes; homework filled the hours until I was back in uniform. Some days I didn't see or speak to my roommates whose lives followed a nine to five pattern. The blue-print I had drafted for re-entering the nursing profession included saving enough money for recertification. That plan was boosted in 1988 when, after the third anniversary of my arrival in Canada, the sponsorship period was completed and the church returned *Búp's* deposit. I had never gone to the congregation for financial help and my sister told me to keep the two thousand dollars. My nest egg started to grow.

School fees were one ongoing expense I did not begrudge. Learning is a lifelong investment. So is immigration. Integrating newcomers into an existing society assumes there will be merging, that gaps exist in the pell-mell pace of the dominant community into which willing arrivals can squeeze. Sometimes I felt that I was missing cues on what to do or which behaviours to copy.

Imitation came naturally to me in Vietnamese. An innate sense of tone and timing had helped me quickly acquire Cantonese. In Hong Kong, people sometimes assumed I had grown up in an overseas Chinese community. Emulating the toneless, uneven syllable-stress of English proved much more challenging. I spent hours in front of the television listening for vocal patterns of news announcers. Using the very valuable bilingual dictionary I had received from the monk in Hong Kong, I generated vocabulary lists with definitions and pronunciation notations. These I studied everywhere, from bus bench to toilet seat. Prompted by pocket-sized notebook pages, I repeated sounds and recited each list for several days before copying out a new set of ten to fifteen words. Every day I built my mental dictionary. When would I know enough? Language was a vast ocean. I was afloat. After my allotted hours of funded English study had been spent, I launched into a much stormier sequel, high school English. How superficial my linguistic competence was became clear in continuing education at Victoria School.

Vic was in transition from its tough, vocational composite highschool history to becoming the city's leading school of the arts. Continuing education classmates included thirty-somethings like me who had risen to the heights of ESL only to land with a thud at the bottom of the barrel where literature, not language, formed the core of secondary school English. Layer upon layer of historical references, cultural nuances, and literary devices seemed far more impenetrable than the demilitarized zone that had divided Vietnam between 1954 and 1975. Several of my Vietnamese acquaintances had unsuccessfully challenged the twelfth grade English exam. While my math and science credits added up relatively quickly, I doubted my hold on poetry and essays. Taking one course a term, I followed a more circuitous route and worked through three preparatory English levels. Short stories intrigued me, providing intensive exposure to quirky, larger-than-life characters, contextualized idioms, and late twentieth century syntax, but other literary genres were academic bling I simply could not afford. Achieving seventy percent on the provincial education department evaluation was bitter; I missed, by ten points, the minimum prerequisite for nursing school. Neither Shakespeare nor Shelley had improved my accent; reading long dead men's words had not enlarged my capacity for charting living patients' conditions. I failed to find the applicability of iambic pentameter to the rhythm of Canadian life. Con Ed seemed like a con, a dead end.

There had been no fast-track back into nursing. Time was ticking along. My medical training was becoming dated. No one seemed to have a way to measure the knowledge in my head or the know-how in my hands, and so, such expertise was deemed non-existent. I felt rejected, discriminated against. What to do? Nursing was the vocation for me. I did not have the luxury of dabbling in this or that, playing with career choices. I had put my head down and worked for five years, salting away my paycheques in order to go back to square one and earn a Bachelor of Science in Nursing.

Meanwhile, Alberta had not been saving much of its oil and gas revenue. Ralph Klein became Premier of the province in 1992. Debt became the foulest four-letter word. Publically funded health services were on the chopping block. Closures of what would amount to half the hospital beds in the province began. The exodus of nurses to the USA swelled when nursing jobs were slashed just as I was on the verge of being able to requalify. But to make the grade for what? If I were to invest four years in full-time studies only to be unemployed, well, I couldn't chance that. My aspirations for another round of nursing education dissolved like palm sugar in a monsoon.

Beyond the Walls of this World

Watching economic and political forces sluice my dreams down the gutter got me thinking. Freedom, I realized, had come upon me unawares. I had been so busy chasing my future that I rarely reflected on the present. While many in the society around me sought attention to affirm the freedoms they cherished, I had achieved a quiet liberty. Canadians moved at will unhindered by minders; it didn't occur to anyone to incessantly check over their shoulder for a watcher. In contrast to countless pairs of eyes ever noticing and noting informable tidbits to trade for favour from Asian authorities, I felt delightfully invisible here. Anonymity spelled relief from being vigilant about who was looking on harmlessly and whose gaze was hazardous.

Over time, to inform no one but myself, I had been consistently concentrating on what other people did well and how they did so; this had become my pattern of unobtrusive learning. Many helpful lessons came to me through people whose friendliness never strayed into intrusiveness. I was free to become the private person I wanted to be. Far from my eastern experience of take or be taken, Canadians honoured giving back. The choice to contribute to the common good built community among strangers who had almost all come from afar. Fostering a shared future by extending an open hand to those who arrived after them moved me profoundly. The contrast to my youth couldn't have been sharper. Across the water, blood relationships had made for big, big obligations in the small world of my childhood. Here, the kindness of strangers made a big city smaller.

The freedom of the city was tempered by a web of dependence. When observing public protesters yelling, chanting, or decrying choices by engines of industry or legislative authorities, I shuddered. Too much freedom felt a hair's breadth away from anarchy. Discord made me very apprehensive. Experience had taught me that executive exasperation easily boiled over with dire consequences; where I came from, anyone could be jailed indefinitely without charge. Innocents might perish. Society itself could shatter. Where I had been, dissenters were squashed like scarlet lily beetles under a gardener's heel. I feared my Canadian-born neighbours didn't behold the bounty or sense the blessings at their fingertips. Were they ungrateful?

Contrary to xenophobic myth, most newcomers did not arrive empty-handed or headed. Our hands were skillful; our minds, chockful of memories, experience, and expertise, drove us to regain the standing we had lost. We worked diligently. If we could thrive, it seemed that any and everyone could prosper. Poverty in this land of plenty perplexed me. Unlike amputees, the destitute or disabled who begged along Asian thoroughfares, here I saw healthy-looking young men beseeching motorists idling at traffic lights with forlorn looks and signs that said, "Buddy, can you spare a buck?" "Help me home to Bay D'espoir" or "I'm hungry, Sister. Have a heart." They had adequate language to ask, and gumption to stand and wave. I assumed such energy was enough to get them through a workday. Surely they weren't all cheats dodging responsibility and scamming a generous system. People naïvely trusted that the existing social and economic infrastructure would always be there, keeping the walls of our world in place.

I knew otherwise. Halted, as I felt, in mid-flight to my vocation, it was too painful to look into the future. I looked back. Had I been born too late? How had I arrived at this juncture just as the metaphorical signal turned red? My wondering mind meandered through the past. The view was different from here. I saw providence not in a safe escape or swift resettlement but in all adversities surmounted. It was impossible to articulate to anyone the depths of my marveling at how far I had come. In my mind's eye, a defenseless little girl, too young and guileless to know better, had set out on a reckless journey. Yet here I was about to take my savings for university to make a down payment on a townhouse. The opportunity seemed to have fallen from the sky into my astonished lap. To me it was nothing short of miraculous that after seven years in Canada, with mortgage rates ever lower, there was a chunk of this earth I would soon call my own home. Advanced education was the end I imagined that I had just lost but, in fact, these life lessons were the means to settling in and beginning to root in the soil of my adopted land. No curriculum could compare to the way experience had been schooling me.

Millions of sisters and brothers in the kingdoms of men had sought escape from villains and tyrants. Some succeeded easily; some struggled. Others died, swamped by waves or pitched into the depths by pirates. My world wasn't so small anymore, as it had been in Vietnam where I peered up and out at it as if from the bottom of a well. The world was wider now than it had looked from Hong Kong where I contemplated freedom, leaping, tumbling, and kicking over the sea and in the sky.

The western world gave pause for more wonder, not less, although who knew, even rarely, how to push pause on its automated answers in order to delve deeply? Inquiring minds seemed outnumbered by acquiring hands. Collecting additional stuff consumed more people than did curiosity about life's meaning. Perhaps there was an inverse relationship between their quantifiable acquisitions and the quality of their curiosity.

Voices in my community beckoned.

"Enjoy yourself! You've been working hard. You deserve a good time. Come out to the casino."

"Spend some money. Dress with flair."

"Party with us!"

Mockers too took pot-shots.

"Your car is trash. Put it in a museum."

Others cajoled. Excused. Crowed.

"Put your books aside. Want to die with a pencil in your hand? Don't be a fool!"

"I've paid my dues, now society can support me."

"Take a look at the rocks on my fingers, the glitter on my wrist, the gold around my neck."

Jewelry had no place on a health care aide's uniform. As for the party-life, a seven-minute cigarette in one hand and as short-lived a man in the other, that wasn't in my blood. I was just a peasant girl still dazzled by the fragrance of fruit blossoms and hanging on to every whisper of the wind. A few stronger attractions faded with resistance. I ignored criticism and reveled in the richness of knowledge, better than jade or gemstones. As I moved out of survival mode toward affluence, the instincts I had been guided by became more articulate. Time seemed short. Some way and somehow, I had to make up for the three years taken from me in refugee quagmire in UN camps.

"All you own is so steal-able," I wanted to say. "People have killed and been killed over swagger and swag. I'll stow what's valuable in my brain."

Ever since I had been a little girl, I recognized a determination to free myself from my mother and to avoid a lifetime up to my knees in paddy mud, baking under the sun. I could see where the idea first came to me. There I was, in pigtails, earnestly bypassing rice fields for the rural school room. What I couldn't discern was the source of such thoughts. How had such single-mindedness taken hold of me? Why did learning matter so much? What was the point of bettering myself? Would striving for improvement never cease?

Accompanying *Mỹ* and *Linh* to the Good News congregation, I heard sermons about the insufficiency of human effort and the vanity of good-works. It was said that the good Lord loved us and sinless Jesus had sacrificed himself for us, but none of these notions lodged in my mind. Neither people in the pews nor at the pulpit connected with my heart. I remained lost and lonely in the house of God. Dressed up in Sunday best, "Hi, how are you?" was still a shallow greeting. Small talk about the weather was not the meat of relationship. One clergyman pointedly asked if I wanted to believe in God. If I had wanted to, wouldn't that mean that I already did? Believe that is. I mean, why would I want to trust someone if I didn't already think she or he were trustworthy? Why would I want to accept as true anything I still considered untrue? To leave wants aside and truly live love, now that would be a rare and daring feat, and as far as I could see, was not on the agenda.

"Is that all there is to know about me?" I mused in response to the reverend's question. "You are assuming that you see whom you are talking to. Do you actually appreciate where my soul is?" Why didn't he say, "I've seen you attending fairly regularly. What can I do for you? Let's chat. What are you wondering about?"

Several years into my Canadian life and I had almost always been in a state of wonder. Those were tough economic times yet my part-time hours blossomed into a full-time position. I felt I had wings to fly while others tripped along, uprooting again and leaving the province, or eking out an existence on unemployment insurance. A side-effect of shift work was silence in shared accommodation, and into those quiet spaces came contemplation. Luck inadequately explained how, in this strange land among strangers, so much goodness had come my way.

My sleep, in contrast, continued to be fragmented by malevolent memories that emerged in dreams. The terrifying visions didn't come nightly, as they had in the camps, but spectres still stalked. Militia, guns drawn, kept chasing, chasing, chasing me down, tracking dogs snarling at my heels. I howled aloud, waking myself to the empty room. There was no one to listen, not a soul I confided in. Other than two teachers, I felt I had met no one worthy of trust, sincere and loving to all she met and in all he did. Try as I might, slumber was elusive after being startled out of such dreadful nightmares. The actual sight of cool and composed local peace officers, appearing along a street or in a public venue, was never a comfort to me. An unexpected encounter with any authority in a uniform toting a billy club and revolver sent a chill up my spine. I would tense as if the beatings I had received after one of my failed escape attempts were about to restart. Instinctively I would slink around a corner putting distance between me and the trigger of my fright.

So, in my solitary, very personal struggle for meaning, I wondered if perhaps my portion of life's hardship had passed, and if I had entered a consolation round. In tranquil hours, I caught a panoramic view of my life from those first, shaky steps off *Đồng Nai* island to the resolute strides taken to escape dying without dignity in some cell-block or homeless on *Hồ Chí Minh* City's streets. In my quest for the essence of existence, I constantly questioned how I had prevailed over death, tossing about over the deep in our peanut-shell of a boat. We had naïvely put our lives in the hands of promise-breakers. Among the survivors were those least fit to last. An anonymous universe wasn't vast enough to answer for the evil I had encountered, let alone encompass the good. Who had kept us keel down? Shielded us from rape and robbery? Coincidence couldn't account for it. Some One had been present, protecting personally, perpetually providing.

With the distance of years, I sensed more and more profoundly that I had been steered through disaster. Every sea voyage by my people had reshaped each boat person. I could ponder these thoughts only when I was alone, in quiet spaces, but never in the crush of a crowded auditorium or the hurly-burly of a church vestibule. Liturgical expressions of reverence couldn't hold a candle to the magnitude of the salvage of broken beings such as me. Conversations after Sunday services commonly veered from the magnificent to the mundane, sacrificial goodwill abandoned inside on the altar rather than altering and animating our lives beyond. The cost of love seemed far too high for many people to pay.

Good Samaritan Inside Out

Every shift at the Good Sam, I served people in physical, emotional and spiritual need who were rarely visited by family members. The residents became my residents. My residents and my compassionate colleagues became like family to me. I woke up eager to go to work where the health of the whole person was cared for. A little extra time to laugh together while pulling up a senior's support hose, or Head Nurse Bev standing arms akimbo sending me home to bed when I came in with any communicable condition, these were the loving touches that bonded us together.

It is a great gift to know love, and to love. It is also a mystery. Metaphors revealed more to me than sermons. One evening I was invited to hear Thomas Stebbins, a guest speaker, whose illustrations distilled the essence of love for me. Out of the mouth of this genial, Vietnam-born American came exquisite word pictures in my own tongue. An unlikely host of Ukrainian Orthodox saints gazed down from sun-lit stained glass in the borrowed sanctuary.

"If it's a hot day, what do we wish for?"

Mr. Thomas prodded, pausing long enough to allow listeners to think.

"What could relieve the heat? Wind? Yes. We breathe in. We breathe out. Can we touch that breath, that wind, the air? It touches us. It is life. Can gold buy such a breeze? Each breath is a priceless treasure."

"Your spirit needs a mighty, rushing wind, invisible except in what bows before it. Your spirit remains strong, not by forever holding breath in but by releasing it, letting it move through you."

"Our eyes don't see God nor do our hands touch God. Yet as surely as our lungs crave the breath of life, our being yearns for the Spirit of God."

My body responded in soul-deep consonance. For ever I had believed in nothing. No answers had fit my queries. This was a sudden "Aha!" as if an algebraic equation I had been trying to solve for ages suddenly resolved into balance. This was a turning point. I saw who had been with me all along but to whom I had been blind. There was new life in God's eternal Spirit.

In a sense, I had begun one new life in Hong Kong, and yet another in Canada. Entering this very material New World had preceded coming into spiritual sight. Suddenly my perspective had been shifted. Would wonders never cease? How had it taken me so long to notice intelligible patterns rather than random flukes? Why hadn't I been able to grasp how wide, how long, how high, and how deep was the love woven into every incident, not accident, of my life?

An inner thirst was quenched. I had encountered not an impersonal cosmic force but the Father of Light whose artistry included numbering the hairs on my head. Everything came together. All of the *An* family, entrusted to my care, were in

God's care. They had made it safely onto our escape boat. That fateful bullet, centimetres off a fatal trajectory, could have been my end, but it had been a beginning. From the hands of a priest, a nun, a monk, even guards, I had received streams of kindnesses. In retrospect, I saw that even in Kai Tak, circumstantial lessons in patience had been granted by the most gracious and longsuffering One. Wondering had long been the complement to my wandering. It seemed instinctive to me as a wanderer on earth to observe the starry heavens and rock back on my heels in awe. Wonder was the catalyst in my search for knowledge.

For days following my first hearing, really hearing a purpose to living, my mind was completely occupied sorting memories. Recollections like multi-coloured jigsaw puzzle pieces slid together, interlocking to my amazement. This unprecedented joy I kept to myself.

Private illumination, however, inevitably beams through fingers, along footprints, and on lips. No flame lasts without airing. Teacher Stebbins' speaking coincided wondrously with my comprehending a mystery. To resolve the inscrutable is a wonder. To bend a ray so that I saw through, not just with my eye was not the work of men but of God. To everything there is a season. It was time.

Figures of speech continued to intrigue me. The historical, first-century gospel eye-witnesses recorded Jesus, master at metaphor: the Door, the Light, the Way, the Word, the Shepherd, the Lamb. There were so many facets to discover in Emmanuel. My faith wasn't in rules or regulations, which at best highlighted my failings. Entirely divine, authentically human, Christ made visible God's fidelity among men and women like me. To be true to God, I had to be true to people. I became acutely aware that faith had little to do with leaps but everything to do with leaning. Just as my short physical stature made team-work essential in heavy lifting at a hospital, so weight-bearing in a spiritual sense demanded all hands on deck. There are no solo ascents on the high road of holiness. Hilda was a model mentor. She cared for the Good Sam residents with all her heart. When we first met, I considered her stern. She pushed herself hard and expected others to do the same. Her unceasing patience with wheelchair-bound Mrs. N caught my attention. I noticed how Hilda held those misshapen, crippled fingers close to her heart and bent next to Mrs. N's lips to hear her demands. She replied with respect and never neglected a detail. She even came in on her days off if Mrs. N. was in a bad way.

"You're different," Hilda commented to me one shift.

Funny, I had thought the same of her. Hilda was uncommonly kind. She opened her heart to Ally, a South Asian trained nurse-turned-nursing-aide, and to me. When I was a casual employee, Ally and Hilda were usually teamed for transfers and lifts. For years Ally listened while Hilda recounted minute details hardly pausing for breath. One of the stories she told was about me. In her self-deprecating style, and punctuated by laughter, Hilda described how she and her husband agreed to take a bed I was giving away. They would have made a second, long, cross town trip to transport it had I not insisted and demonstrated that we could strap the frame and mattress to the roof of their vehicle. From Hilda's lips to Ally's ears, and on, over lunch through Ally to other co-workers, the tale portrayed me as impressively practical and masterfully inventive. In actuality, necessity had always been the mother of my inventions. I had moved house five times in as many years without a truck of my own while Hilda and Norm had stayed put in the same house for thirty-eight. But Hilda intuitively raised others up to be more than they could otherwise be. With unpretentious hospitality, she invited me home to share Christmas dinner with her family. By such acceptance and affirmation, Hilda enabled me to believe beyond my oh-so-instinctive inadequacy. For Hilda, belief was a matter of being and living, more than of mouthing what should be obvious. Faith couldn't be displayed in the cut or color of one's clothing, or by out-ranking lesser mortals; devotion to God was inseparable from serving people.

With trepidation, I began navigating the menu at the Good Sam cafeteria - an allegory for my integration into Canadian society. The only item I could initially identify was soup. So for two or three months I ordered soup for lunch after lunch. In those days, our facility cooks prepared all dishes in-house and the home-made goodness in every bowl or on each plate was raved about by my co-workers. They regularly commended the kitchen staff and complimented the chef before heading back to work well-fed and cheerful. In the cafeteria, I ate at their table yet the etiquette and expectations around unfamiliar food were mysterious to me.

As a child, I had internalized *Bà Ngoại's* assumptions about propriety in private and public situations. Her explicit instructions had centered on the unpretentiousness absolutely essential in a guest. In someone else's home, I must wait and watch. I must seek the humble spot. Once invited in to a ceremony or any festive celebration, a modest seat, on the floor, near the back door, even in an ante-room, would be appropriate. Plopping oneself down in a prominent place near the family's ancestor memorial would be a brash disgrace. Social harmony depended on me tuning my behaviour to a deferential key.

No one had schooled me in mealtime courtesy and customs in Canada. Making myself small, unobtrusive and discreet, I was anxious not to be noticed for making some graceless move. Soup here was served without chopsticks, those most elegant instruments for daintily raising bite-sized portions. How was I to lift juicy morsels off a wide, shallow spoon without slurping or splashing? The cafeteria crockery included no tiny saucers for dipping sauces or blending condiments. I feared embarrassing myself because I didn't know what went with what. Was it customary to smother everything with gravy? Or just mashed potatoes? What was gravy, actually? If I didn't spoon it over the fluffy, whipped spuds, would I be able to swallow them, so bland and textureless? Gagging would be awkward. On the other hand, having no practice keeping several distinct dishes separate on one plate, I wondered if gravy flowing onto the adjacent mixed bean salad might make me look gauche. To guard my dignity, I avoided potatoes.

Sticking to chowders and bisques, not much stuck to me. Straightforward Mrs. Davidson, a nurse whose Scottish inflections marked her as a linguistic outsider too, took note that I always lunched only on soup and said so.

"Iz yer soap enuf?"

It wasn't. Over those first weeks I lost weight but, through quiet observation, I gained a mental manual for tasteful pairings. I noticed an urbane diner could leave the insubstantial soda crackers that melted into mush upon contact with broth untouched in the tiny, crinkly cellophane packaging. Gradually I introduced my tongue to lasagna, Caesar salad, and pierogies. Lasagna – flavourful tomatoes and onion-seasoned, peppery ground beef layered between tasty pasta, topped by a crust with just enough crunch, this became my *plat préféré*. It convinced me that from the kitchens of another smallish country with a long coastline and ancient traditions came a comforting and palate-pleasing cuisine. Caesar salad mercifully arrived fully dressed. I savoured its simple hint of lemon and the pungency of romaine, garlic and parmesan, delighted to avoid the unnerving requirement to choose that a vast selection of vinaigrettes posed for me. Like a sharp-eyed understudy, I mimicked my Polish and Ukrainian co-workers, dressing their traditional dumplings with dollops of this or sprinkles of that.

Not getting the combinations correct continued to beleaguer me. How should I bring a coffee for a colleague? Making coffee palatable seemed an insurmountable task. The array of brews and an almost infinite range of permutations on the ratio of cream to sugar or their sundry substitutes baffled me. My default drink would have been tea but Canadians, or at least their public institutions, didn't serve recognizable *cha*. The cafeteria carried slim, white packets, the same size as those questionable crackers, imprinted with red roses and the letters T-E-A. However, the anemic aroma and flavour of this mahogany-toned liquid didn't correspond to anything grown in Asia. Dusty, crumpled leaves sealed in a sachet didn't steep into a fragrance I savoured.

Of course I never commented on any culinary incongruity I experienced. No one ever asked my opinion and, in any case, outlandishness was as much a reflection of me as of whatever I deemed odd. I found myself wondering again. As in my childhood, an almost steady stream of questions wanted answers. Being the only one I could then ask, *Bà Ngoại* had wearied of my inexhaustible curiosity. Burdened by the care of her daughter and her daughter's daughters, my grandmother likely hadn't seen herself as the wellspring of wisdom into which I constantly tapped. She had no inkling of the significance of brushing off my queries as foolish. A child learns to stifle expressions of interest. She may be taught to look askance at imagination. By the time I was settling into my new life in Canada, I had long learned to verbalize few of my questions. But silence doesn't eliminate awe, incredulity or doubt; it drives wonder deeper. Some of my questions were self-examining. Others went unanswered.

One appealing quality that drew me to Hilda was that she didn't play games with questions and answers. She asked candidly because she truly wanted to know. She replied honestly, without hoarding knowledge or profiting by keeping it from others. I grew comfortable conversing with Hilda. Because I knew she was a woman of integrity, I believed her. Belief is grounded in confidence and reliability and has nothing to do with plunging into some murky unknown. Faith, or fidelity to the immortal and invisible Creator, is inseparable from caring for very visible fellow creatures. Because Hilda's preaching was expressed through her practice, I trusted her. I could see the gospel as a message that should inform my work.

Human frailty and mortality, and the accompanying grief, are constants in an extended care facility. Spending each day with infirm, mostly elderly residents was a perpetual reminder that we don't know our time. No one has got a hold on tomorrow. To live completing all I could each day became my measure of living fully. Since faith is effective only in the moment, there's no way to thrust trust backwards to reprise some past demise, or to project it onto a future loss. Integrity and faithfulness count only now, or never. To love like Christ, as he washed his quarreling disciples' filthy feet, was bound to alter my life. Following Jesus' example wasn't an exercise in making myself better but a new and humble habit

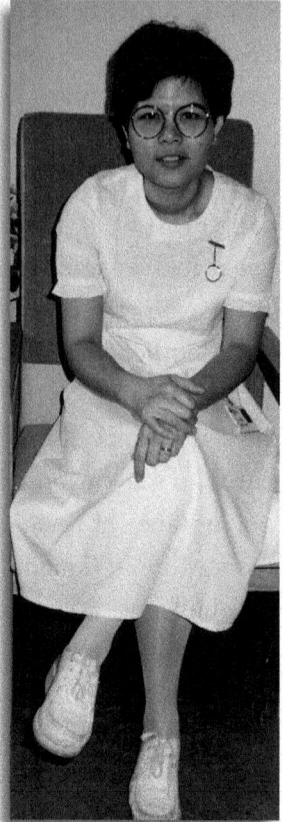

Hanhtiet, 1991, "Good Sam" Auxiliary Hospital

to make others' better off. At the Good Sam, this meant considering each resident in my care as a family member of mine.

Mrs. Minnie was 96 and I loved her. She had endured lean years farming near Stettler and, though failing in eyesight, still saw plenty of comedy in the antics of her fellow residents and the staff. With a chuckle at her own inability to remember or pronounce a name as foreign as mine, she began to call me

China-Doll. Mrs. Minnie thought I was too tiny to support her larger frame during transfers or toileting. She upped her own efforts at using her own strength and, in so doing contributed to her own improved vigour. Although she lacked upper body strength, after folding up the footrests on her wheelchair, she could use her feet to draw her chair out of her room and along the corridors. Mrs. Minnie spoke to me and of me as a decades-old chum from the farming community. I played along. Her family though, became concerned that their mother was really losing it. At every visit with them, she would go on and on about her in-house chum. Her children, seniors themselves, knew of no one from the Stettler area at our auxiliary hospital. One day Mrs. Minnie began to insist that her daughter buy a new red car so she and China-Doll could drive out to their quarter-section to set up housekeeping and farm together. Daughter Verna was sure dementia had set in. Now Verna and her siblings hadn't met me up to that point; the timing of their trips into the city to see their mother hadn't overlapped with my shifts. When I popped into Mrs. Minnie's room that afternoon and was introduced to Verna as China-Doll, I saw a look of illumination in Verna's eyes that matched the sparkle in her mother's.

Some time later, I arrived on the second floor west wing to find Mrs. Minnie quite incoherent and drooling. There was more than Earl Grey in her tea cup. She had topped it up with Irish Cream from a bottle I found nestled among her personal effects in her bedside table. No one had suspected until that day that Mrs. Minnie had been drinking. Almost blind, she had likely poured more than her usual tipple into her Royal Albert Old Country Roses. Verna confessed, when I let her know about the incident, that she was the one who had been delivering contraband whiskey liqueur from time to time.

Verna and her brothers noticed how Mrs. Minnie had bonded with me and appreciated the care she was receiving at the Good Sam. On occasions when their mother wasn't forthcoming with them, or if something came between them, they asked me to intervene. By tapping into her wit, we ironed out relational wrinkles and had pleasure doing so.

We could, in the late '80s and early '90s bolster our residents' social and emotional wellbeing by cooperating tenderly in often circuitous conversations. Forgetful but not forgotten, elders' meaningful interactions unburdened their souls. A human touch in waking, toileting, bathing and dressing five elders could be accomplished before breakfast at a reasonable pace. None of us foresaw that a decade later a nimble N.A. would have to whisk eight seniors, ever more feeble as nonagenarians or centenarians dependant on medi-lifts, through the morning routine in the same amount of time. Great-grandkids, grandchildren, and her own grey-haired children made a splash for Mrs. Minnie's hundredth birthday. She lived to 106, when she no longer recognized China-Doll, but I would always remember her.

My dear Mr. Beatty came to live at our facility after a stroke. Physical rehabilitation effectively recovered the use of his half-paralyzed limbs; more aggravating was his loss of language. Try as he might, Beatty could not get a whole sentence out. But I saw his mind at work and the intensity of his irritation at others finishing his phrases for him. Life partners, thinking alike after years together, sometimes delight in speaking synchronously, but Mrs. Beatty always having the last word wasn't going over very well at all. "Don't let us put words in your mouth," I chided Mr. B, willing his wife to follow my lead. "We will wait for you. Take your time. We will stop feeding words to you. We won't interrupt you half way through a thought."

Daily visit by visit, and week by week, Mrs. Beatty held her tongue as her husband regained his. Whenever he finished a sentence, he would chortle with glee. His cheerfulness was able to bubble out again. The sound of laughter floated out into the corridor telling me a conjugal conversation was progressing well. If he saw me coming down the hall, Mr. B would reach out his hand, a greeting of gratitude. A few months passed and I was about to begin a vacation with my sister's family in California. Mr. Beatty beckoned me into his room.

"I ... will ... miss ... you," he smiled.

Mrs. Beatty handed me a small, wrapped package. Inside was a travel toiletry kit. They knew that I knew that she knew about my holiday plans only because he had been able to tell her. Another triumph worth cheering about!

Leaving took an entirely new tone with a resident we affectionately called Mother Hubbard. To most of the staff, she wasn't merely a glass-half-empty type. The cupboard was bare. She complained that her skin and bones frame was wracked with pain; indeed constantly contracting muscles in her left thigh caused her to hold that leg bent up near her torso. Mother and I somehow understood each other where other aides easily got up her nose. She would eat if I asked her to eat. She would try to unwind and stretch if I suggested she do so. She spent too much time sitting so I encouraged her to loop her arms around my neck, to lean into me and stand on her one good leg. This daily routine prompted someone to capture Mother Hubbard's pirouette on camera. The photo symbolized Mother's clinginess which escalated every afternoon before shift change. Relatively calm through the morning, separation anxiety rose around two o'clock. Loud demands to be up in her wheelchair would be heard. By three, she would have wheeled herself to the elevator I usually rode down at the end of the day.

"Take me home!" Mother Hubbard would cry when she spied me coming, coat, lunch tote and car keys in hand.

"Let's go!" she said as if we were car pooling together.

I squatted down to eye level beside her.

"I've got to leave now. You've got to stay. See you tomorrow."

Tears coursed down her cheeks. Her pleas rose to a screeching pitch.

I took to sneaking out down a back stairwell, feeling rotten about leaving Mother fussing in the elevator lobby. My co-workers joined in, acting as decoys to distract her so she wouldn't notice me setting out from her home for mine.

The knots love ties aren't easily untangled. Orest, on good days, regaled me with stories of his loves or his war. On good days, this World War I vet could spin quite a yarn, even though he recognized he wasn't quite in control of his memories. "Something is wrong with my brain," he would say.

The advance of dementia meant the decline of the man. What was Orest sensing as his mind slipped between clarity and haze? One of the Royal Canadian Corps of Signals, Orest still delighted in the dits and dahs of Morse Code seventy-some years after sending and receiving messages between artillery and observer aircraft in Nord-Pas-de-Calais. But it wasn't victory at Vimy that defined him. The casualties, his buddies, cut down laying cable, riding motorcycle dispatch, or running, those losses circumscribed his heart, perhaps buried it with them in the mud in 1917.

"I can't tell you, nurse," Orest would answer if I probed.

"I'm sworn to secrecy."

He had forgotten many things but never his oath. Orest didn't take vows lightly and had never married although, unprompted and uninterrupted, he told tales of dashing passion and great exploits from times and places I would never know. What I did know was that, once in a story-telling mood, Orest would collaborate beautifully with me as I got him ready for the day, shaved his grizzled chin, or helped him guide his spoon to his lips at lunch.

Cooperation isn't a given between care-givers and receivers. One of the strengths of the Good Sam family at that time was freedom for aides to trade residents where personalities clicked more than clashed. Mismatched is how I felt with Lenora, for example. From my perspective, she was downright mean. I didn't look forward to working with her but I came to see that the change I could affect was in me, rather than in her. For my own peace, I prayed that instead of animosity, love would be sown. On my own Jericho Road, just like the Samaritan outsider in Jesus' parable, any good associated with me was a consequence of grace I was receiving to suspend judgment of broken people, broken like me.

Feast of the First Morning of the First Day

A sliver of the waning moon, the vanishing year, had been visible over the Pacific. *Tết Nguyên Đán*, the Feast of the First Morning of the First Day, was just over the horizon and, in anticipation of celebrating on their native soil, the passengers aboard the 747 burst out in a boisterous and sustained cheer as the pilot touched down on a runway at *Tân Sơn Nhất* International Airport. Flashing "Seatbelt On" signs were disregarded as overseas Vietnamese spilled contents of overhead bins into flailing arms and rushed the door before the jet rolled to a stop. Returning to one's family is the traditional way to mark the Lunar New Year, and other *Việt Kiều* in January, 1997 were anticipating reunions with living relatives and paying respect to the dead. They had gifts to deliver and ancestors' gravesites to tidy up. Among my fellow travelers, some were returning confidently, having left Vietnam as legal émigrés under the Orderly Departure Program while others, like me, had dodged official obstructions to claim asylum abroad. We had been called traitors, American ass-kissers, imperialist sycophants.

Trepidation rather than anticipation described my mood. My separation from Vietnam fifteen years prior had not been amicable; I had escaped a regime that deemed unsanctioned exits not just deceitful and sly, but traitorous. Although I ached for the air, the earth, the rain, the sunset, and the moon, that slighter, silvery moon of my homeland, every subconscious association that broke into my sentient thoughts was of the horrors I had suffered. I was edgy about the reception I would get.

As for families gathering, mine would not. My sister, mindful of eldest daughter duties, had managed to bring our mother, at sixty-seven, to California where *Búp* could care for her. I arranged a meeting with my half-brother, seven years my junior, whom my mother had given as an infant to a childless couple who raised him as their own. I had never before visited *Bảo* or his adoptive parents in their home. A lifetime farmer on *Đồng Nai* Island, *Bảo's* father sat smoking a hand-rolled cigarette as a cat rubbed his bare feet and rested her belly on the cool concrete floor of their home. *Bảo's* mother welcomed me as did his wife. His little daughters warmed up enough through our visit to sit on my lap, but their house was not my home.

I had no home there. That was the hard truth about the places of my childhood. I wasn't sure what I had come to find, but I definitely experienced a new displacement. I was out of step with Vietnam. The homeland of my memory had vanished. Even the language took me aback. Standing alone, each Vietnamese word was comprehensible, definable, useable, but new-fangled idioms stumped me. Unable to follow all the rush and tumble of conversations with strangers or among former neighbours, I sensed a profound estrangement. The outsider I had become accustomed to being in Canada was oddly also the role into which I was cast here, where I had believed I belonged.

My great solace was the affectionate welcome of old friends and school chums. The passage of time had not erased the invisible ties with *Mai Dung, Tuyết, Lý, Phượng* and *Trị*. In our middle-aged conversations, the voices and visions of artless teenagers revived. The balanced one was still steady, the dramatic one still intense, the mischievous still a scamp. All accepted all around.

The other relationship without walls was with Mrs. *Ấn*. It was her husband who came to collect me at the airport and who recognized me after I had elbowed my way through the throng of meeters and greeters. Without the *Ấns* shoring up my resolve, I might never have made it out of Vietnam. Even so, they could not feel, as I acutely did, that the country I had left, had left too. The poignancy of being reunited with these sensitive and always supportive seniors was heightened by a cancer diagnosis for the retired nurse. I made a second journey the following year, to see, speak, and listen to her, before she also left us.

These losses loosened the binding of my soul to the soil of my once-upon-a-time heart land. I returned, rather glum, to my vocation, to care for the elderly whose recollections of yesterday were dimmer than those of yesteryear. Some of them lived half in this world and half in the next. I realized my allegiance was just as itinerant as when I had arrived in Canada a dozen years earlier. At first, the externals had seemed most glaringly different between native daughters and sons, and those born abroad. Then I came to understand that the unseen, unspoken systemic roots of behaviours could also separate me from my fellow citizens. Later still, recognizing that a common ancestry or shared language and culture hadn't fused me irrevocably to a particular patch of Earth, I struggled anew with fitting in. I wondered if I would ever feel right.

Belonging is ultimately an act of the will rather than a response of the heart. This is the conclusion I came to through two spectacularly powerful experiences on subsequent travels in Vietnam. In 2009, I took a tour with the two people who knew me best: my American sister *Búp* and my Canadian friend, Deborah. North of the ancient capital at *Huế*, we passed through pastoral scenes. Verdant fields of rice rippled as the wind whooshed over the paddy. We couldn't escape an incongruous eeriness. Death became palpable to me. I was troubled. The tour paused and the guide pointed out sites with names that seemed vaguely familiar although I had never been in that province before. We came to the *Bến Hải* River which, with five kilometres on each bank, had formed the DMZ, the Demilitarized Zone, during the twenty-one year partition of Vietnam into North and South. The *Bến Hải* had run red with the blood of my people. My people, powerless to avert the deaths of millions. My people, under orders from powers near and far, perished pointlessly. Oh, the futility and horror of death upon death upon death upon death.

War accomplished nothing. Power wore a new face, true, but no transformative wonders had descended upon Vietnamese society in antebellum splendor. I sank in silent reflection under the weight of the unnatural disaster that had befallen my motherland.

It was unnerving, how far beyond lucky I had been. I had escaped injury growing up in wartime. My injuries afflicted in escape had healed. I had found refuge. No harm had befallen me in resettlement. Not once had I felt that Canadians rejected me. Everyone I had met had made space for me. Unlike others, I had never heard directed at me those hostile words, "Go back to where you belong." On the contrary, it was I who wondered how I could ever see Canada as home. Vietnam had been a corm within me where my spirit hid itself against adversity. Her exquisite language rooted me in a thousand years of poetry and patriotism. I had been instinctively protective of that stem and had been hesitant about grafting into a nation quite unknown. The river of blood began to wash that reluctance away.

Amid the springs and waterfalls around Đàlạt, I caught up with a schoolmate at the Trúc Lâm Zen Monastery. In the relative cool and calm of the South Central Highlands, I discovered a beauty that fueled my sense of wonder and moved me through another phase of grieving the country of my birth. Perhaps those magnificent pine forests, the refreshing breezes, and the distance from the hubbub of the lowland cities had prompted Ngô Đình Diệm, President during my early childhood, to select Đàlạt as the site to train the country's youth to serve the nation. This was to have been his legacy project. Service in the common good had been in rather short supply in the toppling and assassination of President Diệm, which had made news even in our backwater village. Without a radio or even a newspaper in my home, hearsay of the November 1963 slaying of the brothers *Diệm* had been repeated neighbour to neighbour. Wandering among the roses, chrysanthemums and orchids of the hilltop gardens in the most exquisite scenery I had seen in Vietnam, I recalled learning of the president's death. At the time I had been too young and far too unsophisticated to see in the shooting a portent of coming calamities. With the subsequent regime change, the American war in Vietnam ramped up. Millions of Vietnamese and American souls were senselessly snuffed out. Hundreds of thousands fled into the future, leaving much unfinished, the import of their lives suspended, unwillingly entangled in a no man's land of the past. Like snowy lilies splayed on a bier, *Diệm's* hope-filled wisdom to unite Vietnamese died with him. I would never unearth the country I was longing for. The home, the land, I had hoped to find was irretrievable. It no longer existed.

Suddenly I was awash in sadness at no longer being part of Vietnam. These were uncomfortable, foreign feelings, being a stranger in the land I called mine. Through the sting of separation, I was being loosened from the great collective which is the culture of my people. On the return flight to Canada, I mused. Detaching my individual present from the communal past had never been my intention, and yet, only as I sensed the subsiding walls of origin could I fly into an unfamiliar joy beyond. So for the first time, I was, in saying farewell to Vietnam, going, finally, home.

$\mathcal{E}$pilogue

At the time of publishing, Hanhtiet is winding down a very rewarding career in long-term care nursing. The precision she prized in childhood play proved to be a valuable transferable skill. *Cô Dung*'s insistence on caring for people in the right way for the right reason has also had its rewards. The people Hanhtiet cares most about have drawn her across borders to walk where her cherished sister walks in southern California, to trip up Via della Conciliazione in Rome when one of two beloved nephews was stationed in Europe, and to stroll with dear ones through Rue Bonsecours in Montréal. *Bà Ngoại* had hardly heard of such places. She couldn't have conceived of her granddaughter running off to a destiny beyond the horizon, or that any good could have come from that. But she did. And it has.

Hanhtiet (L) and Búp, 2020, Edmonton

a bout the Authors

Story-teller **Tiet** is a tender of all things green; her garden flourishes outdoors and in. She is a discerning blender of tastes whose cooking nourishes family and friends. Tiet is a mender of bodies and spirits, of residents who find their niche in golden age care.

Story-catcher **Barbara** credits her first grade teacher for sowing the notion that, since the Creator has given us two ears and one mouth, there's a beautiful balance in listening twice as much as we talk. In the classroom, she has learned far more from language learners than they could ever have learned from her.